An Ulvog Journey

Riverstone Finance Press
Alta Loma, California

An Ulvog Journey

Copyright © 2020 Riverstone Finance Press
All Rights Reserved.

Growing Up Ulvog – Memories of South Dakota, Copyright © 1997 Sonia Strand Pooch. Used by permission.

An Unexpected Adventure, Copyright © 1999 Carl Ulvog. Edited by Peter Ulvog. Used by permission.

Mom's Memories, Copyright © circa 2008 Louise Hofling Sherrick. Used by permission.

Economic Life on a Farm in the 1940s, Copyright © 2019, 2020 James L. Ulvog. Individual articles previously published at Ancient Finance (www.ancientfinance.com). Used by permission.

James L. Ulvog, general editor

First Edition, Second Printing

Published by
Riverstone Finance Press
8780 19th St. #305
Alta Loma, CA 91701

Printed in the United States of America

Cover design by Caligraphics, www.caligraphics.net

ISBN - 978-1-942066-10-1 Print copy
ISBN - 978-1-942066-11-8 Electronic copy

This book is gratefully dedicated to Daniel, Knut, Alfred, and Anna, who made the long, difficult journey to South Dakota from Norway. It is also dedicated to Lydia's mother and paternal grandparents who also travelled to the Dakota Territory from Norway. Because of their daring, determination, and sacrifice, their grateful descendents can enjoy the wonderful blessings of living in America.

Many of Daniel and Lydia's children and grandchildren have labored to see this material in print so that Daniel and Lydia's descendents today, along with those yet unborn, will know something of their heritage.

Cover photographs
Date of family photos is uncertain but was prior to late in 1940.
Front cover:
    Front row, left to right: Carl, Clarice, Gilbert, James
    Back row, left to right: Olaf, Louise, Alice, Daniel
Back cover:
    Front row, left to right: James, Lydia, Clarice, Daniel, Olaf
    Back row, left to right: Daniel, Alice, Carl, Gilbert, Louise

Contents

Preface	1
Section 1	
Growing Up An Ulvog – Memories of South Dakota	3
Gilbert	5
Carl	7
Alice	13
Louise	17
Daniel	27
Olaf	41
James	43
Clarice	49
Section 2	
An Unexpected Adventure	51
Reading About Your Own Funeral	94
Postscript to *An Unexpected Adventure*	96
Section 3	
Mom's Memories	97
Section 4	
Economic Life on a Farm in the 1940s	103

Growing Up An Ulvog

Preface

Why this book? To remember our past.

My dad, James Ulvog, departed this vale of tears on January 11, 2019. After being welcomed home by his Lord and Savior, he greeted his dad Daniel, mom Lydia, siblings Gilbert, Carl, Alice, Louise, Olaf, Lloyd, Clarice, aunts & uncles, many cousins, and a host of other relatives.

He was the last of his immediate family to leave this place for his eternal home. Future generations will not be able to hear from any of that departed generation what their young lives were like.

Their departed voices may still be heard in remembrances gathered by my cousin Sonia. Uncle Carl's delightful storytelling, particularly of his experiences during World War II, may be enjoyed in a book he and cousin Peter pulled together. Life on the farm after grandpa Daniel died can be seen through the facts and numbers found in the probate filing for his estate.

The goal of this book is to pull those documents together so that Daniel and Lydia's great-grandchildren may hear those voices years from now. More importantly, the dream of Sonia, Peter, me, and my other cousins is that generations yet unborn may also hear those voices.

By recalling what life was like in the 1920s through 1940s, all of us can cherish where we came from.

Pondering life then helps us appreciate and treasure the radical advances in technology and medicine in two generations. Life is so much easier today than in the days when our aunts and uncles were growing up.

So, please relax and listen to these voices from the past.

A few other thoughts on this book.

No effort has been made to harmonize the various stories or resolve any differences in recollections that may exist. Those will be retained as written by each of the siblings.

Carl put lots of pictures in his book. Sonia included photocopies of several dozen pictures in her book. I have family photos of life on the farm provided by cousin Sonia.

This first edition will not include any photos. Why? So I can actually get something into print.

I started dabbling on this book over a decade ago and then set it aside until three years ago. Since then I have been working on it with a bit more focus, however, life in general and the need to make a living in particular keep getting in the way of finishing. Because adding all the photos into the text will take substantial time, this book will go to print now. Watch for a second edition with lots of delightful pictures, but please don't hold your breath.

James L. Ulvog
August 2020

Section 1

Growing Up An Ulvog
Memories of South Dakota

Foreword

I am sure some of you are wondering why I took on such an effort as putting this book of memories together. (I have asked myself that in the last few weeks!). I guess it all started last Summer (1996) after 2 trips to South Dakota. I guess I thought everyone knew the stories my Mother (Alice) had been telling me for years about her childhood and places she and her family had lived. Well I was wrong in my thinking! My own brother (David) did not know any of these stories. I then and there decided to attempt to make an effort to "preserve" any memories you all might have about Growing Up An Ulvog. I have tried to be as accurate as possible with the information you have given me. Yes there are some blanks to be filled in, hopefully this can be taken care of at this years reunion. I hope you will enjoy reading what your brothers and sisters have to say as much as I have enjoyed reading this while typing it.

I was interested to see that no one mentioned what a wonderful artist your Mother, my Grandmother Lydia was. But I am sure she never had the time or the tools to do much drawing for you growing up. I wish I had kept the 2 drawings I distinctively remember that she made for me when I was quite small, that of a cow and a horse. Two things I am sure she was most familiar with. She was the only grandparent that I knew very well and loved. She was probably the most patient person I know next to my Dad. I wish I had inherited this characteristic instead of her family's migraine headaches!

I have put this book together as an act of love for my mother and her family. I hope you will cherish and appreciate the words and pictures you will find on the following pages. I hope you enjoy your reading and will share this book with your children.

Sonia Strand Pooch
August, 1997

Growing Up An Ulvog

Gilbert Joseph Ulvog
Born April 26, 1916 – Died December 15, 1983

Gilbert Joseph Ulvog and Ruth E. Elliot
Married April 25, 1975
Children: Theresa, Barbara and Erick

Growing Up An Ulvog

Carl Gerhard Ulvog
Born April 11, 1918 – Died March 29, 2009

I was born-so I've been told-on a farm about 8 miles from Elk Point, SD. This is the same place where my mother was born and raised. There, along with other siblings, I did many of the usual things that rural children did in the process of "growing up". Such as: falling down from an old semi-retired big horse at school. My older brother, Gilbert, would ride this horse to school, and when I began schooling, I would have someone help me up on the "back seat". At recess one day, there was a second farm horse present and a game of horse racing developed. (There was very little racing, just getting those plow-horses to walk was a chore). Like any good "cowboy" I had to "strut my stuff" and had someone put me up on our 20 year old "Prince". He was shaped about like a barrel, no detectable spinal ridge, and I just sort of slid off one side. Prince stopped and when I regained consciousness I was flat on my back under his middle, starring up at his underside. Whoa!

Breaking my leg when a rope on a swing broke, just as I was about to break all records in the height reached by that swing. Hurt bad.

Trapping pocket gophers, along the walk through pastures on way to and from school. The gopher feet got me 5 cents each in bounty pay. Coyote grade school, together with the playground is now gone. Sad.

Picking potato bugs off potato plants and dropping them into a can of kerosene, some of which liquid always seemed to find your clothing. Ugh.

Rolling old big truck tires, sometimes letting them go, by themselves, down a hillside; sometimes with someone inside. Fun, except once when I was "making like the wheel" in a tire that stopped halfway thru a barbed wire fence.

Learning to play the violin (mostly against my will). Practically every Saturday for over 2 years my father hauled me off to a strict and demanding perfectionist teacher. I'm not sure if she ever told me that I played well (I can still remember her baton rapping my knuckles) but I did hear her tell my parents that she had "made a violinist" of me. Unfortunately, I abandoned the instrument and have regretted that for all the years since. (Grandfather in Norway was once a concert violinist).

Chopping down cockleburs and sunflowers in corn fields with a kind of sword or machete on hot humid days. Drudgery.

Skating with only one skate. I don't remember who found the skate, it was a clamp-on type and too big for our shoes so we'd use it pretty much like present day skateboards are (Too bad we hadn't fastened a board on it and had it patented then; we might have been wealthy now!) There was a grain storage building with a low-pitch roof on the farm and we would get up on the roof and coast down on the slope, stopping as near the edge as possible by putting feet down hard. I set the distance record by not putting my feet down quick enough and flew right off the roof. Flight OK, landing rough!

Helping to care for and nurse a baby horse which had been chewed up to near death by coyotes or wild dogs. It learned to nurse by sucking on our fingers in a pail of milk, just like orphaned lambs and little calves. The only difference turned

An Ulvog Journey

out to be that the horse never forgot drinking from a bucket or pail. Even when fully grown he would come to us if he saw us with a pail, and if it was full of milk, he would stick his mouth and nose clear to the pail's bottom, sucking it empty. The snorting sprayed everything nearby with foam. Fun but messy.

Custodian of a white "angora type" goat. A school mate gave me this billy goat together with a harness for it, but didn't explain that it was incorrigible. Our attempted "training" of the thing just deteriorated into the sort of activity favored by the goat, anything where he could use his butting talents. He would take on anything that moved, cows, horses, whatever.

Catching and penning up guinea fowls on cold fall nights when freezing temperatures seemed imminent, a process involving flashlights, long bamboo poles with wire hooks, burlap sacks and enough squalling to awaken half the county. Exhilarating but exhausting.

Being thrown from a six horse-drawn disc-harrow while mulching and burying dead cornstalks and getting partially run over and thus trapped before horses could be stopped. Two hours of digging with my one free hand accompanied by a great deal of "conversation" with the horses (plus much sweating from fear horses would start) made this one of the longest "rescue times" I've ever known. Real nightmare stuff.

Helping with the annual "meat harvest", always in cold fall climate. This would probably rate as the least pleasant activity of all recalled adolescent endeavors; one big fat hog, a big yearling steer and one full grown "bottle baby" lamb reduced to hides, bacon, ham, steak, chops, hamburger, sausages, etc. Oh yes, lest I forget, at one of these events I must add to the above innocent victims, a white goat that stupidly ambushed my father. He was no doubt "shocked" to discover that his very refined "butting techniques" failed to stop an ax between his horns.

Well, you specified childhood experiences and maybe the foregoing carried it farther than you want. However, all this occurred while all of us siblings were together. In those days, adulthood came at an early age, about at 13, 14, or 15 years. So it is at this point in time, about 1933 or 1934 that we, as a family, began to break up and travel different paths.

Carl Gerhard Ulvog and Dorothy Christon
Married August 22, 1948
Children: Peter, Paul, Eric and Randi

Growing Up An Ulvog

(Editor's comment: To be clear on context, this narrative was included in the book edited by Sonia Pooch.)

A brief life history was sent to the Leif Erickson Society by Carl. I have taken portions of this history and reprinted it here.

The man known as Daniel Edward Ulvog in America was born on an island in the North Sea (Norskehavet) November 27, 1884 and was baptized as Daniel Edward Gabrielson, the second child of Gabriel and Andrea Olsen. He lived on the farm with his father and siblings on the island known as Hitra, which is the largest of a group of islands offshore of Trondheim. Much of his youth was spent on commercial fishing vessels. On February 5, 1907 he left Norway as an indentured immigrant to America, at which time he was using the surname Olsen, changing that to Ulvog upon arriving at Ellis Island. His sponsors in the United States were the Andrew Peterson family who farmed in Union County about one mile south of the St Paul Lutheran Church. After serving one year as a Peterson employee (to pay for his travel from Norway) he then continued to operate as an independent farmer until his death on June 1, 1945.

During those years of my youth, I have a very vivid memory of him being: A very industrious, hard-working, self sufficient man, lonesome for the family and friends he left behind in Norway; generous in providing for his family and contributing to church and charitable groups while frugal regarding his own conditions and needs.

I remember breaking a leg when a rope broke on a swing that was being used by me in attempting to set a "height record". My father carried me to the car, took me to the hospital, but had to leave the car about three blocks from it and carried me through traffic and across intersections the rest of the way. After setting the broken bones and putting on the cast, the doctor said it would be nice (not necessary) for me to remain hospitalized for a few days. My father left me there for almost a week. At the time I was having a picnic, but some years later it dawned on me what a big burden this was on my father. Not only was it an expense that he could ill afford (the hospital) but the time lost in the two trips to the big city" was also time needed in field work on the farm. These were depression days.

My father loved music and could probably have done well either as an instrumentalist or singer. One of his earliest substantial purchases in this country was an organ; he taught himself to play it. I remember watching and listening to his playing on Sunday afternoons and on occasional weekday evenings. He was also a presenter (song leader) at church before the congregation could afford an organ-1931. He was one of a group which specialized in harmony (acappella) singing, primarily of the Norwegian folk tunes and comedy songs, at various functions such as Trondelag celebration. The teacher at the country elementary school (Coyote) where I received 8 years of solid basic education, was also musically inclined and felt her students needed a rudimentary knowledge of that art.

To that end she introduced into the curriculum a few minutes of singing al-

An Ulvog Journey

most every day. A substantial number of students took to this extracurricular activity, which became optional and was pursued during recess time. Apparently this group so impressed the teacher with their talent that she decided to form a small band (harmonicas, flutophones, washboards, paper-on-comb, etc.) to perform at PTA meetings and such affairs. I was one of this group, probably in 4th grade or so and thinking I could become the "star" and/or band leader, began pestering (begging) my parents to get a banjo or mandolin for me. Well the band idea sort of fizzled and died (I still have and play the harmonica) and I never got the string instrument pled for. However, not realizing that my father had been wishing (praying ??) for a musician in his family, decided that I must surely be the one. Consequently, one day I was presented with a violin! Although I was disappointed, I did try to learn how to play the instrument, with no indication of progress. My father learned of a semi-retired professional musician in the community and arranged for my lessons every Saturday, 2 hours or more, until I either "passed" the course or was declared incompetent. After 2 years or so, this very strict perfectionist teacher told my parents that she had made a "violinist" out of me. I do not recall her having complimented me on my playing at any time, which may account in part for the fast decline of my playing thereafter. Again, while it was obviously a tremendous burden, both in time and finance for my father to gain this talent for me, I didn't hear any complaining about my squandering of it, but I have spent many sleepless hours upbraiding myself since.

On many occasions, I was astounded at my fathers solution to his lack of finances. For instance, in those by-gone years the common use of horse power (actual horses) for transport over relatively short distances utilized wheeled wagons and buggies when roads were dry. During most of the winter sleds were used and there were various styles and models to be had at a "price". Not having that "price" my father simply made his own by building ski-like devices that would fit on the hubs of different wagons, converting a "lumber wagon" to a bob-sled! Also in those depression and drought years, the common man's motor vehicle (because of cost) was a touring car, so called due to its open body style with a cloth top. These tops flapped badly in the wind and the fasteners holding them together, when new, were soon torn out. To solve this problem my father developed metal frames which could be attached to the doors and lower body panels and to which the cloth parts of the top (called side curtains) fastened with screws. In effect he really invented a convertible sedan. It was much warmer in the winter than the original top. Furthermore, in observing blacksmiths at work and in experimenting, he taught himself the art of welding by literally fusing metals together by partially melting 2 or more pieces of like material and forcing the white-hot points together by hammering on an anvil.

One of my father's loves was horses. He conversed with them as he fed them, while he brushed and currie combed them, during their harnessing and while they worked. He also purchased wild horses that had been caught by professional cowboys on the open ranges of the midwest. Obviously these previously totally free animals had acquired great fear of humans because of their capture and harsh treatment. That my father was able to gain the trust of them and could train them to work for him, is surely testimony of one man's patience and communication ability. Several of these horses had become so domesticated that I and other of my siblings

Growing Up An Ulvog

could walk out into the pasture where the animals were grazing, talk to them, scratch and stroke their hides, pick burrs from manes and tails and hop on their backs for a leisurely ride...no halter, bridle or rope needed. To me this was as close to a miracle as I can know.

Growing Up An Ulvog

Alice Ruth Ulvog
Born July 26, 1920 – Died December 10, 2007

After Mom and Dad were married they managed the "County Farm" where they cared for any and all who were sent there for lack of a home. They lived there till Gilbert was 3 or 4 years old. Aunt Clara worked for the folks while they lived there so that's how she and Knute met up. One thing Mom told us was that she thought Clara never washed her hair as she kept it pinned in a big pile on top of her head.

When we were quite young, Louise and I received identical dolls from Knute and Clara for Christmas. They had pretty long hair and we surely treasured them. However, when we could play outside in the spring, we made the mistake of leaving them out overnite. They were discovered the next morning, they had come to a brutal end when Dad's pigs found them and tore them to bits. You can well imagine how sorry Sis and I were, but we didn't get much sympathy from our parents.

Then I recall my 6th birthday when I awoke to find a beautiful doll with eyes that opened and closed, as well as movable limbs. I also got to go for a ride with Dad to some neighbor and the others didn't go along. Along this vein, I had quite a surprise for my 20th birthday when Dad gave me a huge doll as a joke and that one I kept for some years until I gave it to one of Cora's girls.

We had a happy childhood, even though we didn't have much by today's standards. I don't know how our parents managed to raise 8 of us, but we never went hungry and we had sufficient clothing, food, etc. We never knew we were poor, because there weren't any neighbors who had much either.

We had very few toys, but we sort of made our own games and entertainment. It was fun to try walking on a barrel... rolling it along till we fell off. Also we had a lathe with a cross-piece which we used to roll a metal hoop. We had so many trees to climb, mulberry trees to feast on, and a big orchard.

I wonder if Lloyd can remember when he and Olaf had eaten green plums? It was a scary time, as they became deathly ill. I guess Mom pulled them through by bringing home a cow from the pasture and got some warm milk to give them. They were awful sick for awhile, but thank the Lord they recovered and learned not to eat green plums or apples. One of the places we grew up on was Mom's home place north of Elk Point. (Incidentally, one of Annabelle's boys purchased this farm some years ago.)

On a trip with Olaf we drove in to see if it was as we remembered it, but alas, it didn't even look like the same place. (I was quite disappointed with that.) We had a long walk to Coyote Country School across the fields. Dad took us to school in a lumber wagon if the weather was bad. In the winter time we went in a sleigh. We sure had speedy rides then as Dad drove a team of Broncos. Oofda!

When we were kids we got into our share of mischief. I guess the worst time was when we had been playing some game with a nail keg. As kids will do we left it when it lay in the driveway. So when Dad came home from the field he didn't see it—but the horses went crazy when they hit it. He really had a wild run away. I

An Ulvog Journey

suppose he though us kids might be in the barn yard, so he headed for the grain alleyway. He must have jumped off the cultivator before they crashed. The stupid horses stopped in the hog yard just a little further on. I can still see Mom kneeling by the kitchen window, she was crying and praying for Dad.

Not all of my siblings know about Dad's near fatal run away before our folks were married. He had to work for a farmer to pay off his ticket from Norway. It was while he was mowing, the horses were frightened by something and Dad was thrown from the machine and was hit by the sickle. They didn't know if he would survive as he was cut in his side.

I think my older brothers had a few laughs at my expense when I was quite small. We had geese and the darn gander would chase me when I came any where near their nest when the goose was setting on eggs. Also we had a stupid billy goat that always seemed to know when I came out of the house. He would come running and I would stand and scream for Mom—while he kept butting me. I've never had much love for goats since.

I think Carl will remember when the rope swing broke and he suffered a broken leg. I wonder if he can also recall that Gilbert had a bicycle which he had the misfortune to crash into a tree and got a broken arm. I guess that's why there were no more bikes in our family in the ensuing years. I do recall that Lloyd and Olaf had bikes in later years.

When Gilbert and Carl were in the service, I had the pleasure of helping with chores and some field work. Lloyd and I were given the job of picking corn by hand. This was a mixed blessing as you will soon realize. It was quite a novelty at first...but one day when we were about a mile from home, our horses were frightened by a rabbit! Of course they took off full speed ahead for home. When Lloyd and I arrived on foot much later, there stood the horses by the barn. They hadn't even over turned the wagon. Boy were we mad! Oofda!!

Which brings to mind when Louise had a run away with a hay rack while they were putting up hay at a neighbor's place. I don't know how that ended up, because I was learning how to drive my boy friend's car...and I got so excited that I drove right into the ditch...end of driving lesson!

Back to when we were picking corn...that's when I met Mervin. He and a friend came to see about a job picking corn. Dad hired them both because they would furnish their own teams and wagons. So Lloyd and I were spared all that fun. It was the following spring that Mervin and I started dating and became engaged.

I wonder if Olaf recalls when he fell off a horse and injured his arm. Well of all things, Dad took him to a chiropractor in Vermillion (he really thought this was the best). However Olaf was in so much pain, Mom insisted on bringing him to a medical doctor the next day. What a surprise to learn that Olaf's arm was broken!

The only funeral I recall attending was our Grandpa Ven's. The summer he was dying, the daughters took turns caring for him. So our family was there many nights so Mom could take her turn caring for him. I recall all the cousins sleeping on the floor, usually in the big kitchen. I suppose you could call them "slumber parties" except that we had to be quiet. I have no idea how they cooked for so many people. This was the summer when Carl had his broken leg. He sure could get around on his

Growing Up An Ulvog

crutches...so he was nowhere to be found when we had to go home the next morning.

I've always wondered how the folks kept it a secret when there was a new baby coming. It seemed like when Aunt Hannah arrived to visit us, that quite soon we'd waken in the morning to hear a baby's cry and learn there was a new brother. However, we were living north of Hurley when Clarice arrived on the scene. We came home from school to find we had a new sister. Since that made 8 of us, the folks declared an Armistice...that's the day of Clarice's birthday.

I guess I was a "tomboy" and a copy cat, which got me into serious trouble once or twice. I admired the way Gilbert and Carl could walk along the edge of the huge water tank. So of course I figured I could do the same. Well, I didn't get very far before I lost my balance and fell in. Next thing I knew I was sitting in the middle trying to keep my head above water. Guess what I got for my punishment? I was sent to bed with no supper. Oh My! I wonder if Carl remembers when he and Gilbert had the mumps? The folks didn't want the rest of the family to catch them. So they restricted them to their room. When ever they wanted something they would send a note down on a string from their window. Louise and I had to bring their food and water to their door. I hope they appreciated our efforts. I guess you could say we were "gophers" that summer.

We had a close call one winter night when we lived near Hurley. Gilbert and Carl slept in the hall where the stove pipe came up from the stove downstairs. The boys had dropped their clothes too close to the pipe and their clothes started to smolder. Gilbert woke up and got everyone downstairs or we surely would have died from asphyxiation before long! Gilbert had a mishap while riding in the manure spreader. When Dad drove over a plank in the barn yard gate the beaters went into gear and Gilbert tried to jump over them. He didn't quite clear them, so he had his rear torn up. Mom just cleaned the wounds and applied butter and bandages. He didn't sit down for quite awhile, but he healed up without ever seeing a doctor.

Dad borrowed money from a neighbor so he could build a much needed hog house. This was Mom's home farm, her birthplace. Then when we had a crop failure, Dad couldn't make his payments, so the neighbor foreclosed and we had to move when James was just 3 months old. Moving day at that time was always March 1st.

We grew up without a telephone, radio, TV or electricity...but I guess we turned out okay. We learned to work, since there was no welfare like now days. As soon as the older ones could work out, they had to leave the nest. Also we had a good education in our one room country schools. Those teachers sure had their hands full with 8 grades and no teacher's aides either. We always had a good Christmas program,,, and Santa always showed up too.

Although our Dad was strict, he was also fair. But I remember Grandma Ven telling Mom that it wouldn't hurt him to give us kids a little praise once in a while. I suppose he was raised that way. I guess when Louise and I saw Dad's birthplace in Norway in 1980 we could well imagine how frugal his family had been. It took a lot of courage for him to leave his home and family to come to America. Too bad he never had the opportunity to make a trip back there.

Our Dad taught himself to read and write English. He even learned to type as well. He always spoke to us in Norwegian and we had to respond likewise. I'm

An Ulvog Journey

glad he did or we might have forgotten our heritage. When ever Grandma Ven came for a visit we had to speak it to her also. I remember when our Aunt Anna thought it was so remarkable that we spoke it with a dialect or brogue. It just seemed to come natural to us. I often wonder how my grade school teacher could teach me English, since she didn't speak Norwegian, but she could understand it which probably helped some too.

Lucky Mom was a good seamstress, as she made a lot of our clothing. Louise and I were fortunate as we had pretty new dresses for Christmas as well as our nice Sunday School dresses. I recall we all got new mittens, stockings, caps and even some fruit for Christmas. We never got toys that I can remember, but that would have been a luxury and we didn't expect any. We weren't taught to believe in Santa Claus.

Mom made delicious meals of course, but the sauces and jellies were really special. There were currant and gooseberry bushes in the garden back of the house. She made such good sauce of mulberries and gooseberries, great tasting applesauce, cherry jam and currant jelly...just to name a few. After we moved away from Mom's place we were never lucky enough to have fruit trees. But I do remember going to Knute and Clara's place near Alsen. They had huge mulberry trees. We'd bring sheets and canvases to lay under the trees and shake the berries off. What a job it was to pick out the sticks and leaves so Mom could make sauce. That sure was good eating...wish we had mulberry trees in Minnesota.

We had various breeds of dogs while growing up, at least one or maybe two. We always had one named Sport or Rover, these must have been Dad's pet names. Even our horses had such nice names...Queen, Prince, Lady, and other favorites.

I guess we all knew Dad had a great singing voice. I can barely remember when he sang in the choir at St. Paul Lutheran Church where we were members. But how many of my siblings recall the wonderful songs he sang in Norwegian? I have some of them on records, namely "Johan Pa Snippen", "Nikolinia", "Oleanna", "Halsa Dem Darhemma", "A Janta A Ja", "Kan Du Glemme Gamle Norge", and many others not so familiar.

Alice Ruth Ulvog and Mervin Oberg Strand
Married October 26, 1942
Children: David and Sonia

Growing Up An Ulvog

Louise Dorothy Ulvog
Born January 19, 1922 – Died December 23, 2011

I remember Mom telling me that when I was very small, she found me in the chicken coop, sitting in a tub she had put louse powder in for the hens to dust themselves in, and yes you can bet I was covered with lice. I also can remember going to country school, it was quite common for us to come home with head lice we had acquired from school mates, and Mom had a very fine tooth comb and would put kerosene on our hair and comb out the lice. Good thing at this age we didn't know the meaning of pride!!!

We walked to country school, "Coyote", about 1 or 2 miles from home. We would walk thru the pasture, go by Sam Eidem's on the way to school. In the bad of winter, Dad would harness up 2 of the horses to the bobsled or lumber wagon, as it was called, and with robes and blankets he would get us to school. Dad had a big (anything to us kids was big) black fur coat he would wear and we had our lunches packed in gallon syrup pails. If Mom had made meat from the recent butchering, we would have that on our sandwiches. Or we may have had peanut butter and jelly, we never threw anything away, and whatever was left in our lunch buckets, Mom would put in the warming oven above the stove and they would get toasty warm and we would munch on those crusts and leftovers while waiting for supper, which some nights got very late.

In good weather I often would go out in the pasture and bring the cows home. Many nights we would fall asleep waiting for Dad and the boys to come in from milking and I do remember distinctly one night Dad woke me up and said "Supper is ready". I asked, "What are we having?" "Corn meal mush" was Dad's reply. I remarked, "I'm not hungry". "Well in that case you can go to bed!" To bed I went, but I grant you I was hungry for breakfast—probably warmed up corn meal mush. I never cared for oatmeal, and we ate around a round table, so when those younger than myself sat next to Dad, and there were 4, I quit eating oatmeal and never cared for it since. Dad ruled with a strong arm and what he said went. Alice and I were asked every evening after finishing eating, by Dad of course, to wash the dishes, well we would often say, "There is no hot water", "Then you can do them in the morning"—boy did we smart up in a hurry, because by morning Mom would have them all done. Then Dad got smart and would tell us before supper, to get hot water on for the dishes. Alice and I always had a thing about who was going to wash and who to wipe dishes! Never the less, we had a very good Mom who cooked good, nutritious meals-just one look at me tells that. Getting back to the dish washing, Alice would say I didn't wash the dishes good enough, or that if I was going to wipe the table off, I didn't wring out the wash rag enough, I would just gently squeeze it!

Mom made most of our bread, I wonder what happened to that big pan she set the bread in? I can recall seeing her holding a baby to nurse and the other arm punching down bread. There was no electricity in our home those days, so wood and cobs were used for the cook stove. It was one of my jobs to bring in cobs, from the pig yard no less, and also my job to clean and fill kerosene lamps every day. One

An Ulvog Journey

evening it was almost dark and I hadn't done it yet. Mom asked me "Why do you wait so long to get it done?" I was really getting smart now and I remember answering, "In case tomorrow doesn't come, I haven't done it in vain". OOOHOOO that was bad.

In the summer, Alice and I would get a chance to go stay at Grandma Ven's for maybe a few days to a week. I dearly loved to go with grandma to gather eggs. First to the chicken house, to the granary, then the barn and in some cases to the grove. It was here that grandma would find hens nesting in little boxes or small chicken coops and she would watch them and when they hatched their eggs, she would put a partial covering over the opening, to let the chicks out, and the mother hen would be inside to keep them close with her clucking. The chicks soon became used to this and Grandma would let them all out to do their thing-it was so cute to see those darling little chicks. One time we had brought some in the house over at Aunt Cora's, they lived just a short distance from Grandma's house, and Cora's daughter Ruby (who is now a nurse) was so excited she put the little chicken's head in her mouth and bit it off!! Ruby also was one who would pull temper tantrums and would lay on the floor crying, turning almost blue—it was scary as she would hold her breath! One time when we stayed at Grandma's, Alice and I would dress up using some of Aunt Hanna's high heeled shoes. When Alice was asleep out on the front porch (wearing the shoes) Aunt Hanna took them and sawed off the heels, as she felt it was not healthy for her to walk on heels. Later at home we would put cobs in the thumb of Dad's mittens and put the mittens on our feet and the cob would be the "high heel". My, we were ahead of our time. I think we would also dress up in old clothes we found in Grandma's attic—we made our own fun. When playing outdoors, especially if we had cousins visiting we would pick out our own "tree" and that would be "our" house-come over and visit.

Oh, here I better tell too that we had no indoor plumbing, no running water, etc. So it was the out house for us, including the Sears Roebuck catalogue, we could sit there and look at pictures and day dream of the things we would like to get (but knew we would never have).

Our Mom was a good cook and when there was a baby due (we usually didn't know anything about that, till we came home from school, and maybe Aunt Hanna would be there and tell us, "Shush, there is a new baby in the house".) Mom would have cleaned several chickens and have them hanging in the porch, so who ever, if anybody came to help with the new baby, they wouldn't have that to do.

Also, when we had threshers for dinner, Mom would put on a white, nicely ironed tablecloth for them (and those guys were pretty dirty-but good people) and Mom would have the most wonderful meal prepared for them, so in those days, us kids sort of looked forward to having extra people for dinner, meaning we would get a good meal too. Not that we didn't always have good food, it was just special one year, us younger kids had eaten green plums and especially Olaf, myself, and maybe James, I just don't remember, but we got deathly sick, I do believe Olaf turned black. Goodness, how did Mom deal with it all?

All of us kids were born at home. I remember when James was born, he was tongue tied and Mom had to take him to town to get it clipped. I remember it as

Growing Up An Ulvog

if it was yesterday, he was bundled up so cute, he was born January 13th, so it was probably cold. Now when Clarice was to come to join our family, I must have gotten in on the news, as Alice and I were hoping for a sister and Gilbert always said "No, I am getting another brother". Well that was once we won out, but I left home to get married when Clarice was 7 years old, so I didn't really get to know her too well. I had worked doing housework for some neighbors, Marj and Hank Witt, they were very nice to me and it was just before I got married February 2, Alice went with us to Nebraska along with our bestman, Jerry Ellison who worked with Isadore at the Penney's Department Store in Sioux City. We had 3 different apartments before Isadore left for the Army and I was expecting our first baby who sadly enough died during a breach birth-named her Alice Louise and she is buried in St Paul's Cemetery near Grandma and Grandpa Hofling and sister Louise Hofling Ulvog. Those were sad days while Isadore was gone 33 months out of the 3 years. I did get a job in Sioux City, first in the Sausage Pack at Cudahays and at that time Alice, Lloyd, and I shared an apartment on Grandview Blvd upstairs. I was usually home first so I did the cooking. Those were fun days. Later I got a job at the Arcadia restaurant as a waitress, as I didn't like the harsh language they used at the packing house. I really enjoyed my days at the cafe and sometimes my landlady, Pat Priestman and I would go to dances on lower 4th at a club. Oh my, how I loved to dance and we would walk home after the dance about 15 blocks or so. At one time Alice and I both had sleeping rooms on Nebraska Street across from the Masonic Temple. I learned years later that used to be a "red light" district!!! Mercy!

Getting back to school days at Coyote, I was in the same grade as Dorothy Hofling and Isadore was a couple grades ahead of us. I do remember how he used to wring necks off of birds, etc. and I would think he was pretty tough, not knowing someday he would be my first husband.

From a small child, we were all learning to talk Norwegian well, and when I started school, I was reading a poem in class about July and I mistakenly read it as Yuley. Dad reminded us to always answer him in Norwegian and never to forget it, as we may some day be lucky enough to go to Norway with Uncle Knute. Of course that never happened, but I did have the pleasure of going before Knute died and he had written ahead of our visit and told his friends we were coming-especially on the island of Hitra-so we had people waiting for us.

I have in my possession a wooden box, that Mom used to keep the baby clothes in, I put a cloth cover on the lid and it is one of my most prized possessions, along with the one wine glass that was one of 3 that were Dad's that Mom once gave me. When Dad went to town, many friends wanted to buy him a drink or a cigar, and Dad used neither, so he would I suppose accept wine, and these glasses were used for that. I was also given from Mom the only gift Dad gave her when they were married, rather than a ring he had given her a gold braid necklace with a locket with the initials L D U on the front-their pictures are still in the locket today—I am so very proud.

I remember Mom saying when I was born, someone suggested calling me Lucille and she said "No, then you would have the nickname of Lucy!" and she didn't want that! I think the name "Clarice" was to be after Clara and Mae after

An Ulvog Journey

Martha, who was Dad's brother, Olaf's wife. Oh that makes me think of the year that the King and Queen from Norway were coming to visit the U.S. I told the kids in school, in hopes of getting some recognition, that my Aunt Martha and Uncle Olaf were coming to visit-no one seemed surprised and I often wondered, but I kept it to myself, why more recognition of such wonderful people wasn't much talked about. I was so innocent!

In grade school we had a recitation bench and sat there when our class was asked to come forward for our time. We had such games as Anti-I-Over and Pigs Tail, Ring-Around- The-Rosie and Hide and Seek.

When we moved from our "home place", the teacher had a going away party for us, hot cocoa and cookies and a memory book was made up with each of the students writing in it-such as Roses are Red, Violets are Blue, Sugar is Sweet, and So are You. Going to church and Sunday School were a big part of our lives, as there were no skating parties or bowling alleys then. Mom sewed our dresses, one stands out in my memory, a soft pea green wool with long sleeves and with a Peter Pan collar and cuffs, we had for a Christmas program in church when Alice and I sang a solo, don't remember what song it was, but we sure looked good!!

One evening after school, Dorothy and I were in the school yard picking shrop shire, a weed that had a sweet sour taste to it, and here came a guy, probably a traveling salesman with a team of horses pulling his buggy. He said "You girls had better head for home real fast or I will let my dog out and he is mean!" That was all it took for us to get in high gear and head for home. For us those early years were so special, as we had few close friends to play with. We lost our home place and moved to a rental place, to me it was a new world, until I discovered we still had our friends at St. Paul Lutheran Church out in the country, a few miles from where we had moved to and we attended Peterson School. We lived on what I now refer to as the Talley place, as they moved there when we left to go live north of Hurley, South Dakota and there attended a consolidated school and rode a bus to school. This was the time when Clarice was born. By the time I was in high school we lived on a farm south of Centerville, South Dakota called the Ellis place, I may be wrong on this, it was about 7 or more miles south of Centerville.

This brings me to think of Uncle Joe and Aunt Elsie. I suppose Alice and I were staying at Grandma's and Uncle Ted and Uncle Joe were still there, and so we rode into town with Uncle Joe. In those days if you didn't have money to go see a movie on a Saturday night (10 cents) we would walk up one side of the street and down the other, looking to see if we knew any of the people who were in town. When we got ready to go home at a specified time, Uncle Joe told us to meet him at the grocery store and later waited in the car, only to find out Uncle Joe was seeing (?) Elsie, and would take her home, while Alice and I waited in the car—wondering what took so long???

Well it soon came time to attend Joe and Elsie's wedding held in her parent's home there in Centerville. It was a lovely wedding and we felt so fortunate to have her in our family. Elsie was a great coffee drinking Swede and it was nothing to find half drank coffee sitting in the window sill of the bathroom. In later years after Aunt Elsie died at a nursing home, Aunt Hanna gave up her home after Uncle

Growing Up An Ulvog

Bill had also passed away and came to keep house for Uncle Joe. We first heard of Aunt Hanna's beau when brother Carl broke his leg on a sack swing at home and was taken to the hospital in Sioux City. When he came home he told us Aunt Hanna had a boyfriend named Bill Buist. They never had any children and I once asked Uncle Bill why, and his reply was, "I wouldn't think of bringing any children into this cruel world." I was lucky in that on several occasions I got to stay at their home in Mapleton. I remember when I was 8 years old and staying there, Aunt Hanna took me and got my hair cut in a "boy's bob" and Mom wasn't too happy with that. While staying there I went to my first movie, a Mickey Mouse, and he was riding a horse that separated in the middle and for a long time I pondered just how they would get that horse back together again!!

When I went to high school, in Centerville, where I graduated in 1942, we shared rides with kids in the area and we would wait at the then Schmid's Drug Store. I had a dear girl friend whose Mom and brother (the Parks) had a hardware store. Ruth would go in and get a dime for both of us at noon and we would go enjoy a "cherry coke." Boy, did I ever feel special! That was about the time I started getting pimples on the crease of my chin if I ate too much chocolate. I can only remember a few of those who rode with us, the Buckenbergs, possibly Niame Erickson.

It was when I was 18, or just prior to that in December, I had found a valentine from Dorothy Hofling and I asked Mom, "Do you suppose the Hoflings still live at Elk Point at the County Farm they managed?" Well Mom told she imagined they did. So I sent a Christmas card to Dorothy. They were so excited hearing from us, they wrote and said they were coming to see us, on Sunday, January 19th (my 18th birthday) so we made plans for dinner for them. Isadore drove, only because his dad thought the weather was too bad for him to drive. So here came Dorothy, her mother Dagmar, and of course the handsome and charming Isadore! There is no doubt about it, it was love at first sight! We began dating and it was heavenly—the only boy I had ever dated and of course I was the first in the family to be wed. Those were some fun times. Gilbert was always wanting to know what time I got in at night (or in the morning!), so one time he tied a bunch of tin cans on a string and rigged it up so when I opened the door to the staircase, they all came tumbling down the stairs, waking him and then he would know what time it was! Naughty! Another time, I suppose it was to get even, I had moved Gilbert's bed around and sprinkled it with salt. When he came into the room in the dark, he "fell into the bed." Enuff...

Out on the old home place, us kids used to take an old wagon wheel base, just the wheels and we would take turns pushing each other down the long lane—gee that was fun and cost nothing. If and when we ever asked for toys, Mom would tell us "You have brothers and sisters to play with." Oh yes, we made mud pies. The 3 older, namely Gilbert, Carl, and Alice would use rotten eggs for theirs, but Lloyd and I didn't know that so we went in the chicken coop to get eggs and Gilbert caught us in there and locked us in there. Well—that was not to be, so after a cooling off period, we "got smart" and broke the screen and ran and hid in the north oats field. Ask Lloyd, he will remember!

I don't remember hearing about "trick or treat" for our Halloween events. So when we had our first house on south Henry, we were ready for supper when a

An Ulvog Journey

neighbor knocked on our back door saying "trick or treat." I must have stood there with my mouth open not knowing what she was talking about, so she informed me and we made a quick trip to the store and purchased some apples to give out.

Mom used to hand feed baby pigs that were runts in the litter and I believe at one time even had them in the play pen (if we had one). I am sure we did have a play pen, hard to believe but I can recall when there was a baby in the play pen, Mom would tie a white peppermint in the corner of a man's white hankie, tie it on to the play pen for the baby to suck on and sometimes us older kids, me being one of them, would go swipe the candy!!! How naughty could we get?

When it came time to butcher, Dad would hire Edwin Johnson. I do recall Mom telling at one time Dad had paid cash after one of these times, only to have him come back telling Dad he hadn't been paid. So Dad paid him again and the second time he came back and said the same thing, so this time Dad paid him by check. Mom would lightly fry up pork chops and put them in a stone crock and seal with fat and those chops stayed good all winter, they were really yummy.

Aunt Clara, Uncle Knute's wife, was known for her excellent bread baking. She wore her hair up on her head and if a wasp of hair would come down, she would tuck it up with a hair pin. When she fell and broke her hip, her hair was cut and the story goes she had a pound of pins in her hair, Another thing, she would walk around the house bare footed. They had purchased a new cooking stove, a pretty blue, and she stored her dishes in it in the dining room. I remember as a small child, I thought it was an unusual place to store the dishes, but she thought it was too good to cook on~Alice and I were allowed a few times to stay overnight there, and Knute would buy us animal crackers-ooh did we feel special. He had a cat called "Mitzie" and talked to that cat like it was a real person considering they didn't have any family, I guess that was not so unusual. (They had one child that died in infancy). When they were married it was told me later, that they had planned to have a big family, so had purchased large cooking utensils. It was Uncle Knute who in later years taught me to make his well known "woven baskets". So I am proud I can do that to share his tradition-he usually always sent one with greeting cards. He was still making them in the nursing home.

(Editor note: I am sure all my cousins fondly recall, as I do, receiving those woven baskets along with Christmas cards from Aunt Louise. What a blessing they were. If you still have them in you boxes of Christmas decorations, be sure to take good care of them!)

When I was still quite young, we had a billy goat and the boys would get the goat up in the barn, besides the oats bin and I suppose they pushed him out the big door where the hay was brought in to the loft of the barn-but he survived- didn't break anything, not even his spirit-he was an ornery thing. Guess we finally butchered him.

Do you all remember Inga Meter? Well she had always told Mom she would never eat mutton. One time she was there, Mom fixed some, and she ate not knowing it was mutton- -it didn't kill her, don't know if Mom told her or not.

Do you remember how Dad would handle sour pig mothers? He would put a bushel basket over their head and steer them where he wanted them to go. We had

Growing Up An Ulvog

a mule once too, don't remember what happened to him, unless we sold or gave him away. I used to herd cattle in the summer in the ditches over by Eidems. I would lay under a tree and watch the clouds moving about--how interesting!

I wonder if Alice remembers the black dresses Mom got from Rose and Hanna, Mom would make them over for us. Mom always said we needn't worry about what we wore, as long as they were clean and ironed. We didn't have much, but we got by OK.

When I was in high school I worked after school for the science teacher, cleaning the lab, I think I earned $3.00 a week and I know I purchased a skirt and a jacket. Must have worn it everywhere, as I felt pretty special wearing it. No wonder we learned to sew. When Mom was trying to wean a young one from nursing before a new baby was born, she would put a fur piece in her nighty and the child would get scarred and forget about nursing!!

One of the times Alice and I stayed over at Grandma Ven's, Alice got to crying so bad, so we had to go home-she was home sick-I didn't think then at my age anyone could get homesick, but guess it can happen.

For Mom and Dad's 25th wedding anniversary, I was privileged to model Mom's wedding dress and I have it in my cedar chest. I wonder if I can find a picture of that? I barely could fit into it, so Mom must have been very petite when she got married, cause at that time I was 17 or 18 years old.

Mom almost always made our bread and it was so good. However, when and if Dad had to go to town, he would come and ask Mom if there was anything she needed from the store and if we were nearly out of bread and she could see she wouldn't get any made, she would ask him to bring home a loaf or two of bread-well how we loved that and we would sit and feel the bread, it was so soft-but Dad would say, "That bread is food and to be eaten, not to play with!" and that was all it took to straighten us out. Dad's command ruled.

I am not sure, just where we lived when the horses got sleeping sickness, but I believe it was up by Hurley, South Dakota we lived then. We lost 9 horses that summer! I remember the Bronco mare we had, we had been told if we put her in a type of sling and kept her standing, she would survive, but to no avail. The most dreadful experience of all was when our precious "Queen" died. She was lying out in the yard and I must have spent hours sitting with her head in my lap, thinking in some small way I could keep her alive. Once I went in the house and asked Mom if she thought if I got some milk in her she would live!?! What a weird idea, but I was young and it was the only thing I could think of~yes she also died-she was so special and she had a colt we raised, we called "Charlie". There was also a time, we had a blind mare and Dad finally decided he would have to put an end to her life, so he asked me to hold her halter while he shot her-oofda, what an experience for a young girl. I guess I should add that about the time we lost all of those horses from sleeping sickness, was about the time we got our first tractor, I think it was a John Deere.

When we lived on the Lee place south of town, I helped with the haying up by Lind's place. I drove the mower team and also the stacker team. That summer I got so brown, when Aunt Hanna saw me she said I looked like an Indian. That was when I got the idea, if you wanted to look lady like, you must not be sun tanned. I

An Ulvog Journey

would come in and wash my arms with bleach. Silly girl, but I sure tried.

I wonder how many of the others remember the time that Dad had a run away with 2 horses, no it must have been 4 and they came and ran thru the grain building with the 4 row cultivator, breaking all the connections and leaving the cultivator and Dad on one side and they went thru. What an experience that was! But I never remember Dad whipping any of the horses, they were his friends and ours too. When we would walk in front of the horses in their stalls, if we went by them they would nudge us with their noses, maybe we would have an apple for them.

In the spring of the year after the potatoes came up, we kids had to go out and pick potato bugs off the plants and put them in a can of kerosene-that must have been before they discovered that green stuff we sprayed on the plants. Then in the fall, Dad would dig a furrow and we would go out and pick up the potatoes—guess we had enough to last us all thru the winter. Mom would put carrots in sand to keep and out in the barn, we would keep watermelons in the oats bin.

We were fortunate to always have our own milk and cream, we got so used to it, guess we took it for granted. I remember the bowls of sour cream Mom hand in the pantry. One time I wanted to make a sour cream spice cake, I asked Mom how much cream to use and she said "Oh about a cup full".

When we moved to Hurley, Alice and I both were told in our rooms that as new kids coming to school, it was consistent that we bring treats for the class, so Mom made a batch of brownies for both of us to take. Well-the kids said, "Isn't this nice, no one had ever done this before!?! It just so happened that the 2 who had told us were sisters, boy were we ever taken in--I guess I never liked that girl after that!!!

I remember the cherry trees we had in back of our house-it always seemed so big but maybe at that time it was because I was so small.

Gilbert wanted to catch some flies on the wood fence and he got too close to the wood and a huge sliver went right thru his hand, Mom quickly pulled it out and lathered it with butter before putting on a bandage. Another time he was in the manure spreader when it was in gear and he got his rear end in the prongs and cut him up pretty bad, again, Mom "doctored him with butter".

As a very young girl I used to enjoy sitting in the Catalpa trees in the lane where the cattle went out to pasture—seeing things in a much different perspective than being on the ground.

Oh yes, there was a time Alice and I went for a long days stroll along the river bank, found a monstrosity of a turtle. We were not ready to go home yet, so I took the belt off my dress and tied the rascal up, thinking he would be there when we returned, but he had gotten away—I wondered many times where he went to.

Carl used to trap gophers and cut off the feet for a bounty and he even showed me how to take care of the traps if he couldn't go and check on them. I don't think I made a very good gopher trapper.

Many times our entertainment included going up in the hay mow in our barn and jumping down in the hay—only I several times landed in the hole where they put hay down in front of the dairy cattle and I would look up into the eyes of Mom's Jersey cow "Dolly" with the big horns—the wind knocked out of me and scared to death. I think we also tried swimming in the stock tank—not the right thing

Growing Up An Ulvog

to do.

What was the thing we used to start up? Some kind of engine or generator, all holding hands and feel the shock go thru all of us. What exciting fun we had!?!

Oh yes, the time we were up to the Staums up in the hills and all the Staum kids were having fun, they had pop bottles with colored crepe paper in them and cold water. They pretended they were drinking pop and gave Alice and myself some to drink. We didn't know they held it up to their mouth and let the water go on the ground.

Does anybody else remember Dad loading up the wagon and going out to sell watermelons and also storing them in the oats bin for the winter? Those were the best melons—I am sure we wasted lots.

How about when Dad had barrels of molasses for the cattle—we would put a stick in the barrel and thought it tasted pretty good-why for cattle?

Did I write about the time Alice and I broke our wooden bed from jumping in it ? Dad had told us if it happened again we would have to sleep on the floor with the mice. Well it did happen and all we could do was climb into the white baby bed in our room and both of us slept in that, with our feet sticking out of the end, but we were scared!!!

I remember when Mervin and one of the Powels(?) came to help husk corn for us and Alice was out picking corn too-was that her first meet up with her future husband???

Louise Dorothy Ulvog and Isadore Hofling
Married February 2, 1942
Children: Daniel, Greg, Susan and Isadore
Louise Dorothy Hofling and George Sherrick
Married November 17, 1969

Growing Up An Ulvog

Daniel Lloyd Ulvog
Born September 1, 1925 – Died February 23, 2016

It all began on a hot summer afternoon about 1:00 on September 1, 1925. My mother, Lydia Ven Ulvog told me in later years that I was born during the grain threshing time on my father's 160 acre farm near Elk Point, SD. I was the 5th child of eight that were born into this union. I was born at home.

I don't know why, but I didn't at that early age, like to be called Daniel or little Daniel. Even though I was not a junior, I didn't like that name either, so I became Lloyd Ulvog. I lived with that handle until I was drafted into the Army in September, 1950. After my induction into the military I was known as Daniel L. Ulvog.

My early schooling began at the small one room country school that was called Coyote School. It was about 1 1/2 miles by way of roadway from the farm house where I was born. I was taught early how to save time and miles by following my older sisters, Alice and Louise, by taking a short cut across our fields to save over 1/2 mile each way. Of course we had to cross one or more of our fences on this journey every school day. In doing this I'm sure our poor mother had to do quite a bit of sewing up torn clothing, as I may not have been quite as careful about crawling through the barbed wire fences as my sisters were.

Both of our parents spoke their native tongue, Norwegian, at home so that I could not speak English when I started school. This was more or less a problem at school because our school teacher, Maieme Edem, was herself a norski and taught me among others how to speak English. Until their dying days, both of our parents still spoke Norwegian at home and in later years us kids would answer in English.

My parents lost their farm in the "crash" of 1929 due to a foreclosure by the seller. I believe I went to that first school only thru the 1st grade, as we had to move to another farm that Dad and Mom had rented. This farm was owned by the Talley family, whose father was killed while flying his own airplane. I don't remember where the family moved to, but they had at least 2 children, Jim and Glen, that both went to the same school we attended. This was called the Peterson School, now long gone, and just a gravel pit where the school once stood. The Coyote School house is gone also. I remember a Peterson boy, plus Glen Talley was in my 3rd grade class at this 2nd school. We had a nice walk to this school also, at least 3/4 of a mile by roadway and no fences to crawl thru. What a blessing for Mother!

On the Talley farm there was a good sized orchard, with many apple and plum trees. When the fruit was starting to get ripe, Olaf and I would tag along with Alice and Louise to get our fill of plums. They were suppose to be taking care of us little ones. Well us 2 boys could not always reach the ripe plums, so we ate lots of green ones. We would get so sick I am sure Mom would think we were going to die for sure. Mom would scold Alice and Louise so badly for letting us eat the green fruit, I'm sure they wished they would die. Also when I was very small, Alice was taking care of me and we were out on different kinds of machinery trying out the seats and levers. I fell off a plow seat and hit my forehead on the moldboard of a 2

An Ulvog Journey

bottom plow! When Alice got me back to the house, I had lots of blood all over from a nice gash on my forehead that I still carry today! My Dad had quite a few bee hives near this orchard and us kids got stung more than a few times by the bees. I don't know if that farm was sold or what happened, but we had to move again. It seems like we were there only 2 years. This third move took all of us and our belongings to north of Hurley, South Dakota. It was sad to leave our new-made friends at school as well as all the nice neighbors that we had a short drive from Elk Point. We also had to leave our beloved church members behind from St. Paul Lutheran Church. I was baptized in this great country church, as were my older siblings, Gilbert, Carl, Alice, and Louise. I don't remember where my younger brothers Olaf and James or baby sister Clarice were baptized. Our father had sung in the church choir as well as helping to raise funds to add on to the church building.

Our transportation at this time was in a much used Model T Ford touring car. It did not have a heater, air conditioning-yes in a way it did as it had drafty side curtains that we had to snap into place during cold or rainy weather. This old Ford did not have any type of radio (AM or FM) or stereo or tape player! It did not have an electric starter either. It had to be cranked! It was simple, a little 4 cylinder car that did not have much speed or comfort but did the job.

When the whole family was together in the car, driving perhaps to Grandma Vens for a Sunday visit, Dad would sing some of his favorite Norwegian songs. Us kids better not be fighting or carrying on at those times. Yes there was room in that little car for Mom, Dad and 6 or more kids, but we were 2 deep all over inside. I remember our Dad had a real bear skin coat that he wore when driving this car in the winter times. We had either a cow or horse hide blanket that we covered up with in the back seat. It helped some.

The farm north of Hurley was not close to a country school, so we were picked up by a bus and went to the city school in Hurley. The house on that farm was so small that we really had to double up in the beds. I am sure Olaf and I shared one bed in the same room that Alice and Louise had theirs. This was togetherness!

The only heat upstairs in the cold weather came up the stair-well or the heat register in the floor from the old pot bellied stove downstairs. Do you think we poor folks had an inner spring mattress or a water bed? No way! We had to be content with a straw filled mattress, and most of the time the straw would shift around so that there was not much comfort in bed. No wonder I've had back aches all my life! That is what we had to put up with back around 1933 and 1934.

I remember a real bad blizzard while on this farm north of Hurley. We had snow drifts up to the roof of this 2 story house on the north side! There was hard packed snow that was deeper than most of the fences. Dad, Gilbert, and Carl had to put up fences around the barn yard on top of the drifts to keep the horses and cows from wandering away. Most of the time the horses and cows would not sink into the drifts, the snow was that hard packed!

We lived one mile east of a railroad at that time. After the blizzard was over, we could see and hear (this was flat country) the steam locomotive clearing the track with a big V shaped snow plow. The engine couldn't go much farther than the length of the engine and tender on each run. Then it would back up a good length and make

Growing Up An Ulvog

another fast run at the snow drifts. All you could see on those short runs was lots of black smoke and the snow flying all over. We heard that engine a good part of the day, so you know they had a hard time clearing the track. There wasn't any bus service to school for a while either after that snow. I don't remember where he took us, but I remember Dad hitched up a team of horses to the old bob sled (this is a heavy duty sled with a wagon box on it) and we went someplace on that hard packed snow. We may have gone to town. There was no car traffic going down that road at all.

Us kids had a real ball that winter making tunnels thru the snow. It was on this farm that our Dad, Gilbert, and Carl cut down one of the biggest cotton wood trees there was around. I'm not sure if it was cut because it was so close to the house (a safety hazard) or that we just needed the wood for heating and cooking. Anyway, it was a big job and we burned up all the wood too!

During grain harvest up at Hurley, Gilbert was working for a neighbor. His name was Ed White. Gilbert was tending the huge Avery gas engine that powered the threshing machine. I remember watching Gilbert as he drove this big tractor and thresher behind, when he would make the trip from one farm to the next. I know the rear wheels on that tractor were all of 8 feet high and steel wheels all around. We didn't have a tractor at all, just lots of horses to do all the field work.

At one time Louise and I were trying to hide from Gilbert for some reason. I think he saw us run into the chicken house to hide and he locked the door from the outside. I suppose he thought he had us locked up good. Anyway, we managed to crawl under a fence in the yard outside the chicken house and we escaped. We figured we pulled a fast one on our older brother that time.

I don't recall too much of other neighbors of ours living up at Hurley and can't remember much of the kids we went to school with in town either. It was while we lived there that Dad bought a real automobile. It was a 1925 Dodge, 4 door, sedan. Even though it was about 8 years old, it had class. It too had a 4 cylinder engine (but lots of power) no radio or automatic transmission or power steering. But best of all, it had a heater and real glass roll up windows. This car had heavy steel disk wheels, just like a truck. It wasn't too fast either, but it would get up to 60 m.p.h.! This car was built by Dodge Brothers as it had not merged with Chrysler Corp. as of that time.

With all the snow we had up at Hurley, I just couldn't forget about the sled that was owned by our family. We had to share it with all of us kids. Although there were not any hills to slide down on, we still had fun on that sled. I remember tying a rope on the rear bumper of Dad's car and when Dad was going to town, I would sneak behind the car while he got in to drive off. I don't think I got away with that stunt more than a few times. I would get that sled behind the car and hang onto that rope with one hand and hold onto the sled for dear life. I think that Dad got the car up to 30 or 40 miles an hour on that snow packed road to town. The last time I did that I stayed on the sled for about 1/4 of a mile until I lost control of the sled and went rolling and sliding down the road minus the sled. I found the sled OK and I wasn't hurt much (only my pride) and Dad did not know I had been doing this at all. He did ask if one of us had tied a rope on the back of the car though, as he saw that rope when he was in town. That was the end of my roadway sledding days.

An Ulvog Journey

After Dad had bought the Dodge, he took the Ford apart to make a 4 wheel trailer out of it. Gilbert and Carl were very sad to see this take place. They had driven the old Ford to a gravel pit someplace and proceeded to take it all apart right down to the frame and wheels. Dad left all the stuff in the gravel pit that they took off and pulled the frame and wheels home with the Dodge. Carl and Gilbert thought that the Ford would be theirs to drive and keep. It was a sad time at our house for a long time, but we had a 4 wheel trailer! This all took place about 1934 and we still had that old Ford trailer with the wooden spoke wheels till the mid 50's. I wonder how many people got that much service from a Model T Ford?

Our next move to a rented farm was in the spring of 1935. March 1st was the normal day to move when farmers were renting. I remember lots of hard work to get some of the machinery loose from the frozen ground. It was a big job and lots of hard work to pack up and load everything up in the trailer, wagons, hayrack and pull some of the machinery behind. There always were quite a few trips to make a move from one farm to another. Getting the livestock transferred was a big problem too.

This next farm was about 7 miles south of Centerville, South Dakota. It was one of the "Lee" farms. The Prentiss Lee family owned about 6 or more farms all together in one area. The biggest farm of theirs was called the Lee ranch. It had 600 or 700 acres and were the central collection point of other farm's crops during harvest. The common cost of renting a farm was to give 2/5 of the crops to the owners.

By the time I was 10 years old I was introduced to more chores on the farm. After school, us bigger boys, Olaf and I, had to go out and gather corn cobs from the hog yard. Mother used lots of corn cobs in the kitchen stove (a wood stove) to get a good fire started before she would then put on wood. Dad would feed the pigs lots of ear corn and believe me, those pigs sure did a good job of eating every kernel of corn off the cobs. It didn't take too long for us kids to pick a bushel of cobs, bring it up near the house or put them in the wood shed. Then go back and fill another bushel basket till we had gathered 8 or 10 bushels. Tell this to kids today and they will no doubt think you are telling a big fib. We did not get paid an allowance for any of these chores either. Lots of children in the 80's and 90's seem to think and "demand" that they get paid for helping out with any chores or even for breathing.

When I was growing up, helping out on the farm (girls as well as boys) was a way life. We didn't know or use the "no" word either, when asked to do any of the chores. Our parents used discipline in those days, in the form of a handy little willow branch! And it worked too!

At meal times all the children learned early in life not to put more food on their plates than they could eat. If the plate wasn't cleaned off or we refused to eat food that was prepared, it would be there for the next meal. There was not any waste of food at our home.

We always had a good size garden on our farm wherever we lived. Mom would do lots of canning of fruits and vegetables every fall, so there wasn't very much store bought food at our house. Dad would plow up an acre or more for the planting of potatoes every spring. We would plant the potatoes that had been cut up by our mother so that every piece that we planted had at least one "eye" in it. This planting was always done on Good Friday as our Dad believed that if done on that

Growing Up An Ulvog

day, the crop would be big and generally we had lots of potatoes. Some of those Good Friday plantings were not nice days, some very cold and others were rainy days, but the planting was done anyway.

When the potatoes were growing good, we had to go out to the potato patch and pick off the potato bugs! Whew, that always was a smelly job. Those bugs smelled awful if one was smashed. We most of the time would have a half gallon pail with a cup or two of diesel fuel in it to put the bugs in. That would kill them! If we didn't get the bugs off, they would kill the plants for sure. We didn't have any spraying equipment in those years, perhaps because of the shortage of cash. Also child labor was cheap, there was quite a few of us there and it was not against the law to have kids do some work at that time.

It had to be about 1935 that I could drive a team of horses, although I was too short and not strong enough yet to put a harness on a horse. Our horses were for the most part quite gentle and responded well to our commands. Dad would have me use the horses on a 4 section drag for my first experience. It was always a dusty, dirty job, even though I rode along on a "drag cart" hooked on behind the drag. When the corn needed to be cultivated, I enjoyed driving the horses, 2 on a one row cultivator. The horses were trained well to walk between the rows of corn that we didn't have to steer them until they would get to the end of the field. We would have our hands full by steering the gangs on the cultivator as close to the corn hill as possible. These cultivators had wooden handles to use, to control where the shovels would plow the earth. When the corn rows were long and the day was hot, we would have to stop and rest the horses at the end of the field at least 10 minutes or so. This resting of the horses was one good reason to have a tractor instead, because they didn't have to be rested. A big time saver.

It was on this farm that our father had a real close call. He had been cultivating corn with a 2 row cultivator being pulled with 4 horses. Something went wrong out in the field. I don't know what and I didn't recall anyone asking, but Dad lost control of those 4 horses and really had a run away with them. Every one near the house could hear these 4 horses coming towards the buildings on a full gallop! When they came into the yard making so much noise and the 2 row cultivator with Dad on it, just bouncing along behind, the horses headed straight for the old granary. This granary and corn crib was only big enough for 2 horses and wagon to pass thru the center. All 4 horses tried to go thru there, but when they hit it, the horses, cultivator and Dad all stopped with a big bang! Dad was cut up and bruised badly from hitting the levers in the sudden stop. It was a mess to get the horses out of there and put them into the barn and to get the busted up harnesses off of them. The horses were also hurt, but luckily no broken bones. It took more than a few days for Dad to heal up and then more work to repair harnesses and the damage to the cultivator. We felt so sorry for our father with all of his cuts and hurts.

It was also about this time that a deadly disease called sleeping sickness hit a lot of the animals in that area. We lost 6 or more of our best horses to that sickness in about a year's time. The horses would appear to get weak, then fall down and in a day or so would be too weak to get up again. Then they would die within a week. I remember Dad got several of our sick horses into the barn stall and supported them

An Ulvog Journey

in a standing position with ropes underneath them tied to beams over head. All this work still did not save the horses and it seemed that whatever we and the veterinarian would do to any of the horses that got sick would not keep them alive. This was a terrible blow and a big loss to anyone that had to depend on horse power. All of us on the farm were hurt by this loss, as the horses were all so friendly, like pets, that part of us died when each horse would go.

I believe this loss of horses was a sure fire way to get the farmers to buy tractors. Our Dad bought his first tractor in 1936. It was a model B John Deere with rubber tires in front with steel wheels on the back. Dad did not buy any new machinery for the tractor, but instead rigged up hitches on each item that would hook up to that little model B. I didn't drive that tractor much the first year we had it. Maybe our Dad thought it was too dangerous for an 11 year old to drive. Also I was not strong enough to start this tractor. In order to start this engine, the big flywheel on the left side had to be turned over by hand, no "electric starter" and it took good strength to do this.

I felt pretty grown up when I was 12 years old and was able to throw a harness on a horse and hook up a team to a wagon or a piece of machinery. I was also trusted at times to drive the tractor in the field to help out with the work that always needed to be done. It was also about this time that our hogs came down with a disease called cholera. (Editor note: About 1937.) We lost quite a few hogs and many farmers had big losses also. These were very sad times for us. There some times was enjoyment too. We younger boys loved to go fishing. The Vermillion River was about a mile south of this farm and our property ran down to the river. Olaf and I would have to take James along when we walked down to the river to go fishing, swimming, and digging for clams and dragging home turtles. Yes, we caught fish. They were bullheads, catfish, and some carp. The bullheads would survive the long walk home in the hot sun of summer. We would put the fish in the livestock water tank and then catch them again when we were ready to fry them. We brought home lots of clams too. Mom would crack them open and made real tasty clam chowder. Us kids would always be looking for pearls in the clam shells, but never found any.

We often would drag home a large turtle and throw it in the water tank also. We had one of the largest aquariums around and didn't think anything of it. We had a neighbor by the name of Gust Nelson that would stop by often in his 1934 Ford on Sundays. He would ask us boys if we had any turtles to sell him. He loved to make turtle soup and would pay us up to 50 cents for a big turtle!

Somehow, one of us kids found or was given an old bicycle. I know it wasn't easy to ride as it had no tires on it. The bike had a chain seat and we would take turns riding that (cast off) bike up and down our dirt driveway and out on the gravel road too. We didn't have any store bought toys, so we had to make (or find) things for ourselves.

We had a 1½ mile walk to the one room school when we lived on this farm. This school was called the Riverside School. Our mother would fix us a lunch to carry along to school for dinner time. This lunch pail was a 1/2 gallon syrup pail. Again, no store bought things like real lunch buckets for us kids, but we got by anyway and the peanut butter and jelly sandwiches tasted just as good from the syrup pails as

Growing Up An Ulvog

those that had store bought lunch buckets.

One day on the way to school, I had a real bad pain hit me in my back. It hurt so bad that I could not continue walking to school. I lay down in the grass by the road side for a long time till I was able to get back up and get back to our house. I don't know what brought that pain on, but it had to be from some accident that I had on the farm. I remember one time we were playing up in the barn loft. We would see how far we could go on the rope that ran the length of the highest part of the loft. We would go hand over fist until we got tired and fall down onto the hay. One time I fell onto the hay and rolled right down thru the hole in the floor that was used to put hay thru for the horses and cows. I went right down thru that hole and fell down into the manger and that really hurt! Another time in this same barn, I fell out an open door in the loft and onto the ground in the cattle yard. That was about a 10 foot fall and it also hurt very badly. I never broke an arm or leg, but I may have hurt something in my back to cause the pain. I have had a lot in my back.

My father took me to a chiropractor in Marion, SD for treatments for my back. These trips up there always seemed to be on Saturdays and continued on for a year or so. I remember it cost my Dad $3.00 for every visit, plus the gas the old Dodge would burn. I must have been an expensive kid to raise. I remember the big gun collection that the chiropractor had in his waiting room. He had many old time six-shooters, maybe 30 or more. No doubt my Dad helped him buy some more guns for his collection. This chiropractor was recommended to us by our Dad's brother, Knut Ulvog. Uncle Knut had trouble with his shoulders, from working on his farm near Beresford, South Dakota. He always went to the doctor in Marion and claimed it helped him a lot. After a while, my back pain did go away, but I didn't have much faith in that doctor as I would get that back pain again nearly once a year.

It was in 1936 that our mother's brother, Joe Ven was married to Elsie Anderson in Centerville. Elsie had worked as a clerk in a local grocery store where Uncle Joe had met her. I remember that was one time our Mom and Dad took time off from the no-end of work around the farm to go to the wedding. They both looked so nice all dressed up in their Sunday-go-to-meeting clothes. I don't recall if any of us kids went along, but I know I was left at home. It was a long day and Mother had so much to tell us when they got back from her brother's wedding.

On this 160 acre farm, more than 1/2 of the tillable land was on low land. Every spring our parents and the kids that were able, would plant one huge melon and pumpkin patch on river bottom land. This melon patch was 5 or more acres. There were more than a few varieties of melons. I remember one kind that was called winter melon. In the summer when they got ripe, Dad would put lots of them in our grain bins, cover them up with grain and they would keep all winter. We had melons to eat all winter and into springtime.

These were hard times on the farm. We would help Dad load up our old Ford 4 wheel trailer with a 36 foot box, full of melons. We had lots of them. In the mornings Dad would drive to Centerville with Carl along. They would leave the trailer with Carl, in town, to sell the melons. The big, long ones (20 inches or so) were sold for 10 cents and the big round ones went for 5 cents. Every evening when Dad drove to pick up Carl and the trailer, the melons were all sold. The melons grew

An Ulvog Journey

real good in those dry years, compared to the grain and corn crops.

It had to be in 1937 that it was so dry, that the oats and barley grew so poorly that we had some fields that didn't yield a crop at all! The small change that the melons brought in meant quite a bit at times like that. We had thieves around during those days too. At night when the melons were ripening, some young folks, would raid the melon patch. They would take what they could carry, after eating their fill. Dad didn't mind that too much because they didn't damage what was left on the vines.

Our Dad rented more land those years while living on the "Lee" farm. It was an 80 acre alfalfa hay field. This proved to be much more work for all of us that could drive horses. There was mowing, raking and stacking of the hay, all in that order. This was all done with horse power and lots of sweat on our part. I remember when starting to mow this hay (which was done 3 or 4 times each season) with 2 horses pulling a 5 foot mower, it seemed that we would just never get it all cut. We had 2 mowers going for at least 2 days to cut this big field. Dad was busy at home sharpening the spare sickles for the mowers and repairing anything else that needed fixing. Then at lunch time we would rest the horses for about 1/2 hour while we would eat in the field the dinner that Mom would send along. After watering the horses at a neighbor's water tank, it was back to work, going around and around that field again. It was days like that we slept real good at night.

Dad, Gilbert, and Carl fixed up another old Dodge car that they took the whole body off and they rigged up a hay sweep on the back end of the car. When the hay had been cut, dried, and raked into windrows, we used this old car to bring the hay into the hay stacker. Carl was, most of the time, the driver of this machine, we called the "hay bucker". It was much faster than the horses could do the job, as Carl ran that rig at a fast clip, after pushing a big load of hay onto the hay stacker. He would raise more dust in those runs to the windrow to bring in another load of hay. Dad was nearly always up on the stack of hay, spreading it out nice and even to make a high hay stack. I had the job of driving the horses that it took to raise the stacker, after Carl had pulled away each time. The horses that I drove were hitched to a heavy rope that ran thru a series of pulleys, that would raise the hay stacker high enough, so that the hay on the tines would slide off onto the hay stack. I had to be very careful not to drive too far, else something could break, or move the stacker out of position. There were times when we were doing this operation, some of the neighbors driving past on the road would stop and watch as Carl raced out from the hay stacks to bring in another load of hay. This was something quite a few had not seen before.

Out in these hay fields were many rabbits and they were those big jack rabbits. Us kids loved to catch the baby rabbits and this was the cause of "one of my accidents." It was during the raking of the hay with a bull rake. This was a 2 wheeled machine about 12 feet wide, with many curved tines that would rake up the hay. It was pulled with a team of 2 horses, normally quite gentle horses too. It was after I had stopped the horses, ran after and caught a baby rabbit and got back on the seat, holding on to a squirming rabbit with one hand and trying to steer the horses with the other. That was a mistake. I had dropped one of the lines and the horses got scared and off they went. I tried to stop them with one line, but it didn't work. Now the

Growing Up An Ulvog

horses were going at a full gallop, fully out of control with me trying to stay on the seat. I was a very scared 12 year old and soon I could not hang on any longer and fell off the seat and in front of the rake tines that were in the down position. I was rolling around with the hay in the tines, when all of a sudden the tines raised up and came down again. The tines then caught me by the legs and I was dragged across this freshly cut hay field stubble that really scratched me up good. It wasn't too long till the tines raised up again and I was released from my seemingly death-trap. I don't know who was able to stop these horses or where. Also I don't know what happened to my rabbit, but I was one scared kid and well scratched up! I learned not to try and catch rabbits or anything else while driving horses after that wild ride on the rake. I am sure the horses had done some damage to the rake too before they were stopped.

During haying season, with 3 or 4 cuttings of hay, we had put up quite a few stacks of alfalfa hay. This was a valuable and much needed crop and quite a bit of our share was sold for much needed cash. I remember at least one time when during a summer rain storm, lightening had struck a hay stack and it burned to the ground. There went some of our profits! One summer for sure, Olaf and I would herd cattle for a neighbor. His name was Ben Paulson. We had to watch his cattle so they could graze in the field that had been harvested of small grain (oats or barley). There was no fence next to the corn field and we kept the cattle out of the corn for about 5 or 6 hours each day. For our work we were paid 50 cents each per day. This was a lot of money for poor farm boys in the mid 30's. During our grain cutting one summer, Dad's old grain binder (McCormick-Deering) broke down again, as it had done many times before. Although our father was quite good at repairing machinery, he could not fix the worn out blotter. This was the part that would tie a knot in the twine that went around the grain bundle. Remember, we were poor and our hard working Dad had no savings or checking account, so he did not have the $9.00 needed to buy a new knotter. Dad asked Olaf and I if he could borrow enough money to buy the needed part. Of course we agreed to give Dad the money as we had saved, about $18.00 by that time. I know it kind of hurt both of us kids to give up that much money, but I really think we were sort of proud that we helped out with the grain harvest. We had been saving up our hard earned money to buy some fishing rods and reels like some of our neighbor friends had.

One nice Sunday morning, the whole family was on our way to church in Centerville, riding in the 1925 Dodge car, when all at once a big noise came from under the hood and the engine stopped. One of the pistons has come loose and broke out thru the side of the engine block. I don't remember if we got to church that day, or how we got home either but it was a sad day at our house. Dad got another engine and kept the old Dodge running for a few more years.

We always had lots of chickens on the farm. Mom and Dad would order 1,000 or more baby chicks early in the spring time from a nursery in Yankton, South Dakota, called Gurneys. I know they are well known for their nursery, but they had their own hatchery also. We had an 8 sided brooder house that had to be cleaned up real good and had a kerosene stove going several days before the chicks arrived at the farm. This was a busy time for Mother as I don't think anyone else could take care of those baby chicks as good as she could. Mom would be checking out those

An Ulvog Journey

chicks more than a few times each day to make sure there was plenty of heat, water, and food.

One spring, we had ordered a lot of elm tree seedlings from Gurneys. They were planted on the east side of the house on the "Lee" farm. I know us kids had a part in getting all these trees planted too. This farm had no trees around the buildings at all before this. I remember driving past that farm many years later to see quite a forest there.

Now it was moving day again. This move took us to a farm about 7 miles north east of Centerville, to the "Holmberg" farm. It was another 160 acre farm like the one we had just left. We then lived about 2 miles west of our Grandma Ven's home and I remember in nice spring weather, she would walk over to visit with us. I'm sure Dad would drive her home when the visiting was over. It must have been 1938 when we made this move. We had a one mile walk to the one room country school there. This school was called Morning Star. I went to 7th and 8th grades there.

On this farm I was trusted to drive the model B John Deere tractor quite a bit, although there still was much use of the horses in the fields too. Our corn harvesting was still done by hand and at this place I helped out with that also. It was at this farm when Carl bought his first motorcycle. It was a red Indian, 1939 Scout. This was the only bike in our area, so it was quite a thing to see going down the roads.

After 2 years on this farm, we were on the move again as this farm had been sold and the new owners were going to farm it themselves. The next farm was about 19 miles away, as it was 11 miles south of Centerville. We did not have the cattle hauled on this move, we herded them! Our Dad was in the lead with a team of horses pulling the hay rack full of hay. Olaf and I were behind the herd, trying our best to keep the cattle on the road and out of people's fields and yards along the way. We were not riding horses! We were walking and believe me, that was one long day! When we came to the river, the cattle would not cross the bridge. This was an old wooden floor bridge with the planks about 2 feet apart and the cattle could see the water underneath and we were stalled. Dad had good reason to have that hay along! He would cover those planks with hay, then he tied one of the cows to the back of the hay rack and drove across the bridge, pretty much dragging that cow along. The rest of the herd followed along quite well when they saw one had gone across. This new home of ours was a larger farm than we had before, it was 460 acres. About half of the farm was upland and the rest bottom land running east to the Vermillion River. Dad had purchased another tractor for this farm. It was a big model D John Deere, on steel wheels. Gilbert had been to this farm in the fall to do lots of plowing of the bottom land. The big field on the low land was one mile long. Our Dad bought a corn picker, as this was just too much corn to be picked by hand. We had a few very good years on this farm during the war years when Carl, then Gilbert were both in the Army and overseas. One spring after the corn had been cultivated, we had a few days of heavy rains and the river went out over it's banks and flooded all our low land as well as many neighbor's land also. The corn was about 12 inches high and we lost it all on this 140 acre field. That is enough to make a grown man cry! We had about 40 acres of alfalfa hay on this farm and the rest of the tillable land was corn, oats and barley.

Growing Up An Ulvog

This was 1942 and like other countries, we in the USA were in a terrible world war. I know Dad had written many letters to my older brothers overseas. Several times we received telegrams that Carl had been wounded in action. Then we had a telegram telling that Gilbert was missing in action. Then shortly after that, it was reported he was wounded in action. That still hurt, but it was a big relief knowing he was still alive! It was later we were to learn that Gilbert had been blown out of a foxhole by a German "88", his M-l Carbine had it's stock blown off and Gilbert not only had lots of shrapnel in him, he had a shattered wrist. During his surgery, the doctors were able to save his hand by grafting his wrist bone solid. Although he could no longer bend his wrist, he still had use of his fingers and thumb. After coming back to the USA, Gilbert spent 2 long years in Walter Reed Hospital with much therapy to go thru.

In these war years, we had gasoline rationing. New tires were almost impossible to purchase. I remember Dad bought a newer car. It was a 1936 Ford V-8, 4 door sedan. It had the spare tire mounted on the back of the trunk and had full chrome wheels covers. It was a real classy blue car that had a radio in it that really worked. Before he went into the Army, Gilbert had bought a 1935 Ford that was just like a new one and Dad was instructed by Gilbert to sell it. Carl also instructed Dad to sell his Indian Scout as he didn't think he would ever come back alive after the war, but he did!

The years were going by and in the spring of 1945, our dear dad was getting lots of problems from diabetes that he had with him for years. It hurt Olaf and I a lot when he had an insulin reaction while we were working in the fields and had to get Dad home fast so that he could take his medication. This kept getting worse and finally we had to take Dad to the small hospital in Centerville, where his condition worsened and he passed away on June 1, 1945, at age 61. Dad was born in 1884 in Norway. This was a sad spring time in the Ulvog family. Our brother Gilbert could not get home for our father's funeral. Carl could not be contacted through the mail or telegrams of his father's death. Even the Red Cross was of no help. Carl was always on the move and none of the information of Dad's passing was to catch up with him.

This was a tough year for our Mother and us kids trying to keep the farm going the best we could. I know that Olaf and I could not do as good a job with the crops and the livestock as our Dad would have done. But we tried real hard.

Then in August of 1945, Carl came home from the war and when he got to our house, he first learned that our Dad had passed away. This was a very sad time, not only for Carl, but for the rest of the family as well.

Not only gas and tire rationing, but new cars and farm machinery were very hard to purchase during the war years. We had a big corn crop coming up that year and our old one row International corn picker was just about shot. When Carl came home from the war, veterans had priority on new cars as well as machinery and he saw the need for that on the farm. Carl purchased a new 1945 model A John Deere tractor and a new New Idea, 2 row corn picker that fall and had it delivered to our farm. A few neighbors saw this new machinery coming to our farm and some said they should have had it. Others were offering high black-market prices for them.

Carl, Olaf, and I harvested our big corn crop in style that fall. We also

An Ulvog Journey

harvested corn for more than a few neighbors also, that didn't have corn pickers or could not purchase them. Carl and I also harvested the crop that our uncle, Arthur Carlson had that fall. I helped Carl lubricate that corn picker on a very regular basis. It didn't take the 2 of us very long to grease the whole machine, so the 2 of us stayed with that rig till the harvesting was all done. This extra corn picking brought in $5.00 per acre at that time and helped Carl get some of his investment back from the machinery.

Then in 1946 this big farm was up for sale and we had to move again. The next farm was very small, but it was a place to live and keep our livestock fed. It was only 80 acres and had belonged to the Ben Nellis family. Ben had passed away the same year that our Dad had. We stayed there only one year.

Olaf had bought a 300 amp Hobart welding generator while at this farm. I helped him when I could and we built up a 2 wheel trailer to mount this welder and a 6 cylinder Chevy engine to drive it. We were now in the welding business! We did our own repairing and Olaf did quite a bit of welding for the neighbors, sometimes in the field where their machinery broke down. We built up more than a few 4 wheel trailers for sale.

Our next move took us north a few miles on Hwy 17, 7 miles south of Centerville. This place was 7 miles from Wakonda, South Dakota. This farm belonged to the Anderson family, of which our Aunt Elsie, Uncle Joe's wife, was a member. This was a 360 acre farm, of which our machinery was quite capable of doing the work.

It was now 1947 and our brother Gilbert had come home from the hospital. Carl didn't stay with us on the farm long, as he went to Rapid City, SD to enroll in the School of Mines and Technology. I remember we went to Carl's wedding out in Rapid City after his graduation. I know the whole family could not go, because someone had to stay on the farm to take care of the cattle, chickens, pigs, etc. I know Mom and I went there and it was a long trip across South Dakota. No expressways were built in 1950.

The closest to being killed on this farm was in 1949 during the corn harvest. Lots of farmers were hurt badly, loosing limbs or their lives in many different ways with their machinery. I was driving our model D John Deere tractor pulling the 2 row corn picker when I had a brush with death or dismemberment! This old tractor had a nice steel platform between the fenders and right next to my left leg while sitting on the seat was the power take off shaft. Now this power take off had a shield over it, but the shield did not come all the way down to the floor. It was about 6 inches above the floor. I had been wearing a fairly new pair of blue jeans with the cuff rolled up. The universal joint on the spinning shaft caught my left pants leg and some instinct made me stand up very quickly. In the next instant the shaft had pulled my left leg hard against it and ripped off the left half of my jeans. This was very fast undressing! If I had not stood up as quickly as I did and braced myself, very likely the shaft would have pulled me right down to the floor and killed me! I was a very sore Ulvog, but lucky to be alive. I managed to unhook the tractor and drive it home. I was so sore on my left leg, that I couldn't do more corn picking for a few days. Before I drove that tractor again, we had made the safest shield for the power take off shaft that could be found.

Growing Up An Ulvog

It was on this Anderson farm that I received greetings from the President of the United States! It was from President Truman and in the form of an induction notice. This guy was going to take me away from the farm and family for 2 years and he did! This was due to the Korean "Conflict" and I served my 2 years and received an honorary discharge, as did my 2 older brothers. I was now a civilian again! Two days later I married Terry.

Terry was from Chicago, where I served the last few months in the Army with the A.A.A. This stands for Anti-Aircraft-Artillery. I served in the 40 and 90 MM units. After our wedding in Chicago, we left on our short honeymoon trip to Wisconsin, thru Minnesota and then back to my family in South Dakota. This was a very new way of life for my wife, living in the country. For me to start farming would take much machinery, of which I did not have the funds to purchase. I took several jobs, including operating a D-9 caterpillar bull dozer on the Gavins Point Dam project at Yankton, South Dakota. The next winter we lived in Sioux City, Iowa, where I worked next at a meat packing plant. The work I had was hard, shoveling beef or pork into huge grinders. Then I made more money by carrying beef halves into refrigerator rail cars, but that was tough!

We heard from Terry's brother that there were better paying jobs at the Steel Mills in Chicago. In the Spring of 1953, Terry and I said good-bye to Sioux City and packed up all our belongings in our 1951 Studebacker Champion and headed east. We rented a small apartment and I started working for US Steel as a truck driver. This steel mill was not small, it covered 575 acres and employed 13,000 people when I started there in 1953.

Our family grew larger by one, when our only child, Glen Alan was born on November 25, 1954. After a few more moves, we bought our house in Calumet City, Illinois, in September of 1960. We have lived here since then and I did manage to work 31 years before I lost my job at US Steel due to cost cutting. I have been on retirement now since January of 1984 and am enjoying it very much. But I miss South Dakota.

There has been much sadness in our family, so many deaths, but the worst of all was when our dear Mother passed away in 1974. A mother is very close and if you still have one, be very nice to her, tell her you love her while you still can. I can't do that!

Daniel Lloyd Ulvog and Theresa Wisneieski
Married September 27, 1952
Children: Glen

Growing Up An Ulvog

Olaf Kendall Ulvog
Born June 9, 1928 – Died July 30, 2018

When James was a toddler, maybe 2, he was playing in the hayrack (hay wagon) at the northeast corner of the barn on the Lee place. Mother looked out (or was watching) as a small tornado lifted the rack with him in it, off from the running gear (the wheels) and set it on the ground alongside as neatly as could have been done by hand (and back power) and he sat there and kept on playing. We had a wooden silo on the west side of the barn. It had been taken down and the 6 ft deep hole it stood over (dug in it increased the silo capacity) was filled with 4 to 5 ft of very stale, stinking water from rain. I was walking near the pit when a cow with long horns and a small calf came up behind me, hit me full speed, before I knew what happened, I was neck deep in that smelly slop.

Lloyd had his new blue jeans stripped off him by the power take-off on the "D" John Deere while picking corn with the picker. He came to the house with one split open pants leg wrapped around him. Another time while wearing new jeans he had a run away with the horses on a spring tooth hay "buck" rake. He fell in front of the tines and was rolled for some distance, some how got thru them and then was dragged by the pants cuff.

I was told, that I almost died from eating green plums, Mom said she ran out and got fresh milk from one of the cows to pour in me, which no doubt saved me. She said I had green running from both ends.

I was also told I was stampeded by cattle in a barn. I remember looking up and seeing a cow's front feet coming down on me (like 1,500 pounds). I was also dragged by one leg caught in a stirrup when I was thrown from the saddle when the spooky horse slipped on some wet rocks and fell on that same leg, then got up before I could get my leg out...I was dodging hooves.

I remember having several gas tanks blow up while I was welding them, (I've kept my Guardian Angel busy).

I've no other recollections, except the great impact Mrs. Disbrow had on my life, may she rest in peace. She gave me my first pet a gray-white male cat (we had no cats!) and she gave us our first (and probably only) Christmas tree in about 1935.

Olaf Kendall Ulvog and Anna Louise Hofling
Married February 9, 1957
Anna succumbed to liver cancer on May 1, 1958

Olaf Kendall Ulvog and Mavis Wraspir
Married February 27, 1960
Children: Sarah and Mark

Growing Up An Ulvog

James Carroll Ulvog
Born January 13, 1932, Died January 11, 2019

I remember, in the late 1930's, living on the Lee farm south of Centerville, during the drought, seeing corn growing only knee-high (on an adult), and the oats crops failing. Later when crops did grow, having sleeping sickness kill most of the horses that were used for farm work. Then getting an old John Deere "D" on steel wheels to use for power. Dad growing watermelons on the sandy bottom land. When they were ripe, harvesting a wagon load and the next day, our Dad leaving and driving northward to sell the melons wherever he could, not coming back until the load was gone, to have some cash income.

During early cultivating of corn crop, going along with Dad on the one row, horse-drawn cultivator. Watching the dog chasing jackrabbits, it was so dry they'd both leave a cloud of dust—and watching little "dirt devils" swirl across fields.

Going to first grade at Riverside School, 1 1/2 miles by road, most of the time Lloyd, Olaf, and I would cut across the fields. Usually I was a long way behind getting home or to school. Walking thru snow in winter was tough for my little legs.

During what must have been the coldest days of winter, going down on the bottom to the grove and cutting down trees for firewood. There were no chainsaws. Trees were cut down using big 2 man cross cut saws, then cut into lengths that could be lifted up to tractor mounted saws. If trees were too big thru the trunk, holes would be drilled and the trunks would be blown apart with dynamite. After trunks had been cut to stove length, wood was loaded into wagons and hauled home to be split. I was too small to help much, but I had to go along to "help."

In the summers, I usually got to go along to town (Centerville) when Dad had to get some repair work or parts. Most often I could end up getting a nickel ice cream cone at the Rexall Drug Store.

Going shopping on Saturday meant a trip to the creamery to sell cream and taking eggs to Bailin's Grocery Store to get the essentials like coffee, sugar, flour, spices, etc. with Mom. Flour came in 50 pound bags, as I remember, as did chicken feed, and all sacks came in pretty colorful patterns, usually enough of each pattern that several dresses or shirts, blouses and skirts, could be sewed for whoever needed some.

I don't know how our Mother had time to do everything that she had to do. Just some of the things that come to mind are:
- Churning butter by hand—we got to help
- Sewing clothes from the feed sacks.
- Washing clothes every Monday, rain or shine or snowstorm, etc. To start with, water was heated in or on the wood kitchen stove starting on Sunday night and lasting thru Monday. Then loads and loads of clothes thru the Maytag washer, run thru ringer into rinse water once or twice, wrung out and hung on clothes line outside, and brought in before dark and put away.
- Ironing later with "sad irons".
- Baking bread virtually every week, and occasionally a cake or some cookies

or pies.
- Getting up every morning by about 4 and getting stoves all going and coffee ready before anyone else got up.
- Then breakfast ready by the time early morning chores were done. A full dinner at noon and a full dinner at night, whenever everyone got there, all 365 days a year. Plus extra big meals for threshing crews in the summer.
- Cleaning all the milking utensils and the cream separator morning and night.

Not to mention: cleaning the house frequently without the benefit of a vacuum cleaner, mending clothes, monitoring kids bickering, keeping lamps and lanterns clean and fueled, doctoring us when we were sick, fixing lunches for us kids every school day, and doing it all without the benefit of electricity or running water for many years, stretching extremely limited income so no one went hungry and keeping all us kids in clothes.

A late fall or early winter event every year was butchering a hog, and sometime during the year butchering a beef animal, and whenever they were ready (big enough) butchering enough roosters to last a couple meals. Since we didn't have a refrigerator, large quantities of beef and pork were kept at a locker plant in Centerville.

Every spring our Mother ordered baby chicks from Gurneys, several hundred and the mailman delivered them, 100 to a box. They had the run of the kitchen floor that was covered with layers of newspaper. Boxes and boards were their boundaries. Water and feed placed where the chicks could eat and drink. Kitchen kept warm with the cooking stoves. Then each night the chicks were put back in the boxes to sleep and keep warm. This probably lasted for about a week. Then the chicks graduated to a kerosene heated brooder house.

Many moving days--big events--if on school days, we missed most of it. Livestock usually got hauled by Uncle Art Carlson. But everything else got loaded in wagons and hayracks. Getting furniture set up, especially beds, had to be done in one day. Things like farm machinery took longer. Equipment on wheels was hooked up one to another into a train-like assembly and pulled by car or tractor to new home. Livestock feed had to be moved too, like corn, hay, oats, but since it was spring, supplies were fairly low. The total moves must have taken close to a week.

During WW II - rationing- needed ration stamps to buy many scarce items. Stamps issued periodically, like monthly, quantity based on family size. Some things rationed were: car gas and tires, food items like sugar, coffee, meats; some clothing items like shoes, hosiery.

I remember after Louise was married, when we visited Isadore's family running the "Poor Farm" near Elk Point, Mom usually got some extra stamps for shoes, sugar and coffee since most of the "patients" didn't need as much. Before rationing ended, Lloyd buying an old car at Ben Nellis' auction so we would have more stamps for gas and tires, plus to use the car for farm work in the fields. I think he made a pickup out of it. I think it was the first car I learned to drive even though I had been driving tractors for quite a while.

Hunting pheasants during and after the war.

Growing Up An Ulvog

Harvesting potatoes from the garden in the Fall.

Mom's flowers and plants-Christmas cactus, hollyhocks and Four-O-Clocks, rhubarb, dill and winter onions.

Picking gooseberries, mulberries and wild plums.

Dad planting wind-break trees.

Quick Glimpses:
- Weeding the huge gardens—weeds always grew well.
- Milking cows by hand, morning and night.
- Running cream separator, feeding calves milk afterwards.
- Feeding the hogs and chickens corn and later picking up the corn cobs to use for stove kindling.
- Making sure there was enough wood ready to put in stoves.
- Carrying water for washing, cooking and drinking, and for hogs and chickens. Sometimes for garden too.
- Cleaning out cattle and horse stalls and hauling manure to fields.
- Bringing in milk cows from pasture for night time milking.
- Gathering eggs--getting pecked by "clucks", hens who wanted to hatch their eggs.
- Sometimes finding a hen hatching a batch of chicks. Sometimes not finding until hen brought the chicks out.

Other Activities:
- Mowing and raking hay, then stacking.
- Planting and cultivating corn and soybeans, first with horses, later with tractors. Helping seed oats by broadcasting seed.
- Weeding corn and soybeans, mainly by chopping the sunflowers and cockleburs out of the rows.
- Spraying crops for creeping jenny.
- Morning glory and creeping jenny vines in small grain, breaking boards on grain binder reel.
- Shocking oats, later threshing, putting oats in bins or hauling to town.
- Doing chores before and after school, sometimes not done before 9 at night. Carrying lantern for light.
- Grinding ear corn for cattle feed.
- Years of grasshoppers destroying crops, helping Dad put out poisoned bait around field edges to try to stop grasshoppers.
- Milk cows sometimes getting mastitis and not being able to use their milk until they got well.
- Feeding calves from buckets of milk.

After war was ended, one of the neighbors, Clair Hesla, giving me a pair of high leather boots and some uniform pants and jackets that I wore constantly until they were all worn out!!!

Walking after mail, half a mile away, during summer at Ellefson place.

An Ulvog Journey

Carl getting home from war and getting on top of list and buying a John Deere tractor and a corn picker. Then going off to School of Mines.

Mom and us four youngest going to Rapid City for Carl & Dorothy's wedding, and some of us going back again for Carl's graduation. Drove out in 1936 Ford.

Gilbert being seriously injured in Battle of the Bulge and being hospitalized at Walter Reed Hospital in D.C. Later coming home and being given a 1947 Olds by V.A. Car had "Hydramatic" automatic transmission since Gilbert's legs were badly injured. I got the car when I went into the Air Force.

My being able to go to high school, finishing in 3 years, spending last year in Sioux City living with Louise.

Before we got electricity, taking a battery from car or tractor to hook up to house radio so we could listen to evening news and weather on WNAX, Yankton, listening to "Whitey" Larson. Sometimes I got to listen to the "Lone Ranger" and F.B.I. programs.

Helping Dad build feed troughs for hogs and feed bunks for cattle; building a grain wagon box out of tongue and groove lumber; helping shingle a grain building and helping build a new outhouse.

In early years of school, being so thrilled when I could take my lunch in a gallon syrup can as a lunch basket.

Home haircuts. School and Sunday School Christmas programs.

Always having a dog and barn cats.

Seeing my first play, at about age 9, on stage in Centerville, black face actors in "Old Man River".

Tagging along wherever Lloyd and Olaf went. Sometimes in summer going down to Vermillion river to fish, look for clams, or just play in water.

Alice and Louise going to High School in Centerville; later Alice working in Centerville at the Dairy Farm and getting a Gurnsey heifer.

At about 5 years, playing in the yard with sheep and the goat butting me.

Guinea hens in trees, bringing in when blizzard came.

Mom usually having ducks and geese, and my seeing and playing with the little goslings.

Going along with Lloyd and Olaf herding neighbors cattle in ditches for 25 cents a day in late 30's.

In all my early years of school, having an upset stomach 2 to 3 times a week until county nurse took me to Sioux Falls for an eye exam and getting eye glasses. Still getting sick when riding in car and looking out the side windows. Later, in Air Force, carrying a barf bag and getting sick on almost every flight. Didn't gain much weight then!

Shoveling out driveways and paths to barns, etc. Drifts were sometimes 8 to 10 feet deep.

Getting new overalls and shoes when school started each fall, going barefoot all summer.

Doing with hand-me-downs most of the time. Presents for Christmas and birthdays were usually needed clothes.

Sundays, other than doing essential chores, was resting, studying, reading,

Growing Up An Ulvog

going to Sunday School and church, playing and going visiting close relatives.

Big family get togethers in summer, lots of kids to play with and lots of food, must have been 50 to 75 people at some events.

Picking field corn in summer to eat because we didn't usually have sweet corn, then feeding cobs to horses that ate them all up.

Helping drive the horses for picking corn by hand and later on driving horses for mowing and raking hay. In my early teens, going on threshing runs, loading bundles of oats on hay racks to haul to threshing machine.

Getting a sled when I was about 10 and using it to haul feed and water for hogs, cows and chickens and hauling wood to the house for stoves. On Saturdays and Sundays, going sliding on hills.

Learning to ride on neighbors' bikes, we didn't have one until I was about 15, Lloyd bought one at farm auction.

After evening chores and supper, reading, studying or playing games by lamplight. Between chores on weekends sometimes brought play time for the 3 or 4 youngest. Lots of times, other then winter, it was a lot of cops and robbers or cowboys and indians. No toy guns, any stick or a corn cob would do for a gun. Sometimes we had homemade guns that shot rubber bands made from old tire inner tubes.

We had a few games. A few I remember were checkers, "Rook" and "Old Maid", marbles, Pick-Up-Sticks and a Kaleidoscope. We also built model airplanes from kits. We made kites. We played hide-and-seek, "Fox and Goose" in winter, tag, tick-tack-toe and hang man. We made whistles and pea shooters from goose quills. In winter, we had snow ball fights. Rolling old tires by pushing with a stick and seeing how fast we could run with them.

Catching the school bus for Wakonda for 7th and 8th grades and first 2 years of high school

Spring spelling bees--I did pretty well.

Spring floods on Vermillion River bottoms, water as far as bluffs on other side. Ducks and geese flying in as water receded.

These are my random remembrances of my early life, not in any particular sequence. They were times of hardship, hard work, but always love and fun.

James Carroll Ulvog and Betty Mae Radigan
Married May 29, 1955
Children: James, Douglas, Richard, and Dawn

Growing Up An Ulvog

Clarice Mae Ulvog
Born November 11, 1935 – Died May 27, 2004

Clarice Mae Ulvog and Art Patterson
Married 1953 (?)
Children: Robert, Rodney and Carl

Clarice Mae Ulvog Patterson and Eugene Monahan
Married August 10, 1976

An Unexpected Journey

Section 2

AN UNEXPECTED ADVENTURE
By
Carl Ulvog
1998

This autobiographical sketch is dedicated to my wife, Dorothy, without whose persistence and assistance it would probably never have been prepared. Thanks are also due to those in whose company I was involved during the five year period discussed and were helpful in this reconstruction. Also I would like to recognize my son Peter who transferred the typed text to computer format and added the pictures.

Recognition must be given to authors and their research as follows:
Robert J. Raynor: "The Army and the Defense of Darwin Fortress"
Robert G. Webb; "The Coyotes: A History of the South Dakota National Guard, Revised"

AN UNEXPECTED ADVENTURE
INTRODUCTION

This is one person's record of some experiences during the 1940 to 1945 era. Many books have been published to tell the story of this turbulent and violent period. I intend to avoid the broad statistical and detailed history, referring to it only as needed to provide a background. Actually the overall view, the "big picture", was never seen by the enlisted man, and probably not by lower ranking commissioned officers either, while various actions were underway. As Tennyson put it 150 years ago: "Theirs is not to reason why, theirs is but to do and die."

CHAPTER ONE
How it Began

There was a war raging in Europe, America's military strength had been reduced to dangerously low levels, and a "Selective Service" national draft (compulsory military duty) had been prepared. At age 21, and having been employed in various non-draft-deferred occupations, it was obvious that I was highly vulnerable for an early call up. Therefore, together with other neighborhood friends of similar ages and circumstances, I volunteered for the stipulated one year of service. The big recruiting slogan, "Get in now and get your one year over with" was so popular and so successful that no draft calls were made for the first three months of the draft law.

An Ulvog Journey

Unknown to us at the time was where we would likely be sent or what branch of the military we might be in, but our 'gamble' was that by enlisting simultaneously we might stay together. In this it turned out we guessed right.

All of the National Guard was very understaffed so the first volunteers and draftees were assigned there, and in our case, we went to the nearest Guard unit, being Battery F, Second Battalion 147th Field Artillery (FA) Regiment stationed at Vermillion, South Dakota. In 1940 and 1941, all of the National Guard clothing and equipment (except trucks) was World War I age. Guns were actually French 75mm and were used by 147th FA until the newer American 105mm replaced the WWI models in mid-1942.

Colonel Kenneth Scurr was commander of the Second Battalion. He served with the 147th FA in 1940. He commanded the Second Battalion most of the time at Darwin and in the East Indies.

The National Guard was mobilized November 25, 1940, and the 147th was ordered to undergo training at Fort Ord, California, All of the equipment and most of the personal belongings were loaded on trucks, trailers and caissons. Many of the personnel traveled by rail, but I was assigned, along with Art Sammelson, to drive a prime mover, a big Dodge 6x6. On December 5, 1940, we departed, bigger trucks towing howitzers or caissons, small trucks towing trailers. Thus did Battery F leave Vermillion, never to return.

Other 147th batteries, from their respective armories, were similarly loaded and joined the convoy, or we joined theirs, at various stops, so it must have been quite a sight. I do not recall the number of vehicles involved but there were 18 of the howitzers and at least that many caissons. Often we could see some of the convoy over a mile away. Apparently there were some real traffic jams, especially in larger cities such as Albuquerque, NM and Barstow, CA, which I remember. At one point a civilian auto, in the process of passing the column in piecemeal fashion, cut into the column and collided with a towed gun and narrowly escaped being hit from behind by one of the big trucks. The gun barrel came through the car's windshield but no one was physically injured. Mentally, I'm not so sure. We camped at or near towns every night and made the 2500-mile trip in 12 days.

CHAPTER TWO
Fort Ord Days

My camp days were spent, to the degree possible, in a sort of "marking time" fashion. That is, although marching, firing range practicing, learning both howitzer and small arms operations and maintenance, etc., I did not try to be outstanding in any way. I assumed, because of the one-year enlistment, I would shortly be a civilian again and would realize no advantage from this training. Accordingly, I volunteered for, and obtained the position of Camp Detail driver. In those days the army operated on a system whereby the groceries, clothing maintenance, hardware, etc., was purchased and/or contracted for through the Mess and Supply departments, each controlled by non-commissioned officers. I drove the officers to nearby towns, mostly Salinas and Monterey, where needed materials and services were obtained.

An Unexpected Journey

Consequently, in collusion with these officers, I often missed "dressed up" formations, inspections, marching for high-ranking officers' reviews, etc. Furthermore, it meant many town visits, more enjoyable than camp routine. As the need arose, I would take a detail of assigned men into the wooded hills around camp where we gathered firewood for the stoves in our tents. Yes, even in sunny California the winter nights get cold.

Obviously the position of Camp Detail Driver offers no promise for promotions, "out of sight, out of mind", but that was of no consequence for me, ie. only a 'one-year job'. Thus, for someone like myself, used to real physical labor on farms and in highway construction, this turned out to be the "easy" way to go, and I decided military life was not nearly as bad as first feared.

I had a motorcycle that I kept parked behind my tent, except whenever leave permitted my absence from camp. Many weekends and three-day passes found me happily touring the coast area for several hundreds of miles in all directions. I often went to Los Angeles for visiting relatives and friends, as well as sightseeing. Some of these tours proved to be very interesting, a few even exciting, but all educational. One such is particularly memorable.

I had been in Los Angeles again. Departure for camp was quite late Sunday and I suddenly remembered I was to be on guard duty that evening. No big deal, I thought, just "spur my steed" a bit. It could go 100 mph or more. At one of the many small towns along highway 101, I came upon a long line of slow moving cars, probably moving at the village's posted 35 mph speed limit. Having a clear view of the road ahead with no on-coming traffic, I passed that caravan at probably twice that speed or more, only to realize a highway patrol car was in the lead. Nothing to do in that situation except try to get away, which I did for a few miles. Then I saw a clump of trees or bushes along side a dirt road, about 1500 to 2000 feet from the highway. There I tried to hide. Unfortunately, the patrolman noticed the dust raised and casually cruised to where I was. Knowing I would likely be sent to the guardhouse when I did get to camp, I was prepared for the worst. To my amazement, the patrolman simply passed his hand through the heat waves over the cycle, smiled, and sat down in the grass by me. Conversation was on the order of: "Running from or to camp?" Me: "To camp." "Must like it, eh?" "No, sir." "Well, would you like to pick up a few bucks along the way?" "Yes, sir." "OK, just follow me, stay behind this time, for a few miles up the road." There at a weigh station were two huge tractor-trailer trucks overloaded with raw lumber. Marked on the timbers were the load levels allowed. The patrolman said all I had to do was throw off all that was above those markings. Fearing I'd be very late getting to camp, but more afraid of refusing, I said "OK" and thanked him. Not one word about my speeding! Without gloves, throwing a few tons of long, rough, green lumber off those trucks on a hot Sunday afternoon made this unforgettable. The truck drivers paid me and I was on my way. When getting to camp very late, I was surprised and overjoyed to learn the patrolman had reported my detention to help clear the weigh station and requested no punishment for me. Also my name was removed from the guard duty roster! I call that "winning one".

Maneuvers and firing range artillery practices involving all the personnel were common, probably monthly, but I kept no record of these. (Out in one year,

An Ulvog Journey

remember?) Nevertheless, two such maneuvers are impressed upon my memory. One involved simulated battle conditions on the sprawling King Ranch in southern California in mid June. I was a driver of one of the prime movers (gun puller) and, as such, was required to hide the truck and camouflage if needed, near the gun after it was properly positioned. In a nighttime move, being hot, dirty and tired, I just threw my GI bedroll on the ground alongside the truck and slept on top of it. Sometime later the air turned cold and, half asleep, I crawled inside the bedroll. As luck would have it, some kind of venomous creature, probably a scorpion, preceded me into that "GI sack" and objected. I really didn't notice the sting or bite until after the call came for my truck and, half awake, I threw the bedding into the truck and started driving. Then the pain in my buttock near the hip really got my attention. After getting hooked up to the gun, I jumped out of the truck and called for a medic who soon had me in an ambulance. I landed in a hospital in Los Angeles. If I saw the name of it, I didn't make note of it, nor the date, which must have been in the third week of June. I was in a room with a boy (man?) about my age named Mickey Rooney. He seemed to think my predicament was hilarious and joked about it with some of his visitors.

After surgery, then release from the hospital and back at camp, I did correspond with Rooney, who, I suspect, did not believe that I really was in the U.S. Army. This led to an invitation to a party. I was able to accept, and attended in Los Angeles, where apparently a few of the partygoers thought I was something of an attraction, maybe a "weirdo". One of the girls (ladies?) insisted on a picture of herself with me, in uniform, by my cycle. Shortly thereafter a copy of that picture was sent to me at camp, which I passed around to my "compadres" who had been skeptical of my story. Unfortunately, this picture, along with most of my personal papers and other belongings were lost as later activity developed. At the time, however, it got me a good deal of ribbing about my dating a "movie queen". At later reunions of the 147th FA someone usually brings up the subject.

On another maneuver in late August to practice war-games at Fort Lewis, Washington, a totally different event became unforgettable. On the way there and back we camped in small two-man tents at a park at or near San Francisco, close to the ocean. This is when I felt the coldest in my life. In spite of wearing our woolen winter uniforms and heavy wool overcoats, we were shivering and turning blue when the fog and mist rolled in from the sea. Furthermore, while in the field action at Fort Lewis, the weather alternated from cold drizzles to dark cloudy downpours. Consensus was: Surely we are being trained for duty in Alaska.

It was probably a hint that those "one-year enlistments" might not be honored. When we were offered leave [furlough) from camp in late summer and early fall, most, including myself, asked no questions, just took off and ran, even though we were concerned because we were really looking forward to discharge. I went home, of course, didn't even make a note of it, but I believe it was for a one-week period in late September.

An Unexpected Journey

CHAPTER THREE
Goodbye California

On November 16, 1941, almost exactly one year after being involuntarily switched from militia status to U.S. Army is, of course, a very notable date for me. Without being alerted to the why and wherefore, we loaded everything at Fort Ord onto the motor vehicles (much like at the Vermillion exodus) and departed, again never to return. In unloading on the San Diego docks, it became obvious we were not being discharged. The destination at that point turned out to be the quarantine station at Angel Island. As if to impress us, the boats or small open ships transporting us, cruised near the shores of Alcatraz Island, from which prison no one had ever escaped alive. While on Angel Island we met and visited with American servicemen who had been stationed in Manila, had declined reenlistments, and were being brought back to the U.S. for discharge. From the lectures by our own officers concerning customs and living conditions, together with movies and slide shows proclaiming the easy and pleasant life of Manila, Singapore and Hong Kong; and further hearing in person from men who had been there, we were literally "raring" to go. It had all the earmarks of a great vacation ahead.

On November 27, 1941 we landed at Pearl Harbor and tied up alongside a Navy ship, USS New Orleans, which was shortly to be sunk. I do not recall how long we were there, but shore leave was offered on a rotating basis to all of us, eight hours at a time. I, like most, took full advantage of this, and we proved to be typical goofy tourists, sending home souvenirs and cards saying, "Having a wonderful time, wish you were here, etc." We shipped out of Honolulu at night about December 1 or 2. I was too surprised, awaking and seeing water all around to note the date, although by now, I and others were 'beginning to see the light', i.e., enlisted men were not given information, only orders. Rumors were that next stop would be Guam. The Japanese raid on Honolulu on December 7, 1941, found our convoy on the high sea between Pearl Harbor and Guam, of course. Shock and frustration hit all of us, even disbelief. No armed ships in the convoy and apparently no one, except the Japanese, knowing our location, and nothing to see except water everywhere. Radio transmission was immediately stopped, as submarines could pick that up, but we listened to broadcasts telling us all the frightening details, not only about Hawaii, but also of the destruction on Guam. It is doubtful that anyone not actually caught in a situation like we were in could imagine the dread and consternation of a bunch of South Dakota farm boys dreaming of a great Manila 'vacation' awakening to such news. Nobody had to remind us that Japanese warplanes flew over us and their submarines passed under us. That was a terrible feeling on a beautiful Sunday morning.

CHAPTER FOUR
We Sail The Ocean Blue

Up until December 7th, weather had been warm but not irritatingly hot and the sea was relatively calm. However, the ship hauling us, Willard Holbrook, was an old freighter converted to a troopship of poor accommodations. Bedding, if it

An Ulvog Journey

could be called that, was canvas about 6' x 2½' suspended by rope lacing in a pipe framework hinged to steel posts anchored to the floor and ceiling. These 'cots' were mounted in groups of 3 or 4 in such a way that when unoccupied could be folded upwards. The lowest or bottom cot was only 3 or 4 inches above the floor when lowered. There was barely enough space between the lowered cots for a normal sized adult to turn over, provided an overweight person was not in the cot above. If one lay on his back, either the head or feet, or both, rested on the pipe frame. Practically the entire ship's upper hold was full of these contraptions, and of course, there were no windows (portholes) for light.

There were open latrines and showers, probably one for 20 or 30 people. Low power electric bulbs provided gloomy depressing light. I spent very little time in that dungeon, preferring the open deck as many others did. At one time, the fresh water supply was nearly exhausted and no fresh water was routed to showers or latrines, only ocean water. Furthermore, the drinking water was rationed. Bathing in salt water must be tried to be believed; few of us did it more than once. This fresh water crisis coincided with hot weather and rough seas. Many of the troops were seriously ill and 'feeding the fish' was common, but I did not become seasick or feel the effect of meager drinking water. Sitting on the deck amongst many ill men and watching shadows of the ship's rigging form slow circular motions did nothing to cheer us up either. Submarines had been detected and forward motion of the convoy changed to circling as an evading tactic.

When we crossed the equator we held "rites of passage" as required by Neptunus Rex. The polliwogs (those who had not sailed across the equator previously) were blindfolded, led before King Neptune and his Queen, charged with some imagined misdeed and sentenced. Punishment was either a shampoo (a head-on blast from a fire hose), walking the plank, (dropping into a big tub of water), or kissing the Royal Baby (which turned out to be somebody's bare bottom), or some combination of these. It was hilarious, everyone got plenty wet and also everyone received a certificate from the King.

Because our unarmed convoy, literally 'sitting ducks' for the Japanese, had no defense, those ships which carried weapons which could be fired from the decks or riggings, had troops bringing guns up out of cosmoline (thick grease) storage in the bottom holds. On the Holbrook's deck we cleaned the howitzers and machine guns and prepared them for action by tying them to the deck railing and riggings. Empty oil drums were thrown overboard and when they had floated away for some distance, became targets for direct fire. It had all the markings of old pirate days and probably even less effective, as much ammunition went wide of the targets. Getting those guns, especially howitzers, cleaned and fastened for firing meant lots of work for lots of troops and perhaps kept some from simply going mad. Also all of the ships were in their usual peacetime colors and commercial markings. Fearing attack from enemy surface, air or sub-surface vessels, camouflage was in much demand. The solution? Let troops, sitting in rope slings hanging over the railing proceed to slap on gray paint while the ship kept going; some fun, with the ship bobbing and rolling from wave action, which often left a painter hanging out away from the ship's side, and an occasional high wave splashing him; I think those who volunteered were paid.

An Unexpected Journey

I declined painting but watched the aerialists who did a surprisingly good job.

As it turned out all the labor and worry (fear?) on that 'cruise' was for nothing, but I am still haunted by the thought: "Why were we not sunk?" The Japanese ruled that part of the world then. If we had stayed a little longer at Pearl Harbor we'd have surely been sunk there. If we had left there earlier, or not stopped there at all, we would likely have been at Guam and sunk there; unless, worst case, we had reached the original destination, Manila, just in time to join the Death March.

CHAPTER FIVE
Down Under - In a land that time forgot

On January 6, 1942, we awoke in the port of Darwin, Australia, tied up at the only pier or jetty large enough and strong enough for servicing ships of the Holbrook's size. Beginning next day was the unloading of freight but we troops were not allowed to leave until January 13th. Of all the miserable weeks we had spent aboard that ship, this was the worst because here, not only was land close by, but also physically attainable. A quote from the diary of our officer, Colonel Scurr, explains the problem:

> On docking at Darwin pier we were brought into contact with Australia's highly organized dockworkers . . . Our plan on landing was to unload our (14,800) ton ship ourselves as rapidly as possible in (the) face of (an) imminent threat of invasion and bombing. The 'wharfies' regarded the arrival of this convoy as a bonanza that would keep them going forever and refused to permit the use of the dock equipment by any but themselves. We allowed them to proceed one day, when it became evident that their system of rests——'tea-o's,' (and) smoke-o's'——and limited loads, were such that it would take 6 months for them to unload our ship alone and there were . . . others in our convoy that must be unloaded. We pleaded emergency due to imminent invasion but they would make no concession from their peacetime 'make-work' practices. We then prepared to take over the dock by force to accomplish our own unloading.

The standoff was finally settled with the help of the Northern Territory governor and Australia' Prime Minister. Otherwise, this could well have been our first combat experience of the war. It was a happy bunch that left what had been our 'home' for 53 days. One of this group, a 147th FA poet 'wannabe', Selland of Battery D, provided this farewell:

> I have heard of slave and pirate ships
> In poems, songs and books
> But they really can't compare with this
> Stinken ole Holbrook
> The quarters are so crowded
> You can't hardly move hand or toe
> You swear you can't stand it,
> But there's nowhere else to go,
> As long as we live,

An Ulvog Journey

We will never forget the ride we took,
On the crowded, dirty troopship,
The Stinken ole Holbrook.

We actually saw little of Darwin town at this time, as we had to set up camp out in the woods ("Bush" of Australian description). It would be nearly impossible for anyone not experiencing such 'camping' to visualize our situation. Because the original destination was the well-developed Army base at Manila, the cargo in our ships included none of the usual 'comforts of home', such as beds, furniture, lights, etc. Consequently, we made our own from whatever was available. Beds were pieces of wood driven into the ground with a 3'x 6' frame of logs or tree branches wired on top to which wire netting was fastened. Most of these cots or so-called 'beds' were about 2' high, possibly so ordered for uniformity. Initially, extra clothes (few), personal affects and side arms (primarily 45 caliber Colt pistols) were hung in small trees or on stakes near the beds. Later some of the artistically inclined developed elaborate tables and chairs. I preferred to devote any spare time to digging and banking my foxhole or trench. As it turned out, the 'comfort' provided by my 'elaborate diggings' far exceeded the pleasure or usefulness of furniture.

We erected baths by placing empty oil drums, ie.55 gallon iron barrels on platforms of tree branches tied to trees at a height of 8' or so above the ground. By attaching pipes of different lengths to the bottom and drilling small holes at the plugged ends away from the barrel we had a shower for 4 or 5 men at a time. I did not know then where these makeshift water tanks came from nor how we came to possess valves or various sizes and lengths of pipe. Likewise the source of the obviously pre-owned wire for our beds was unknown to me, although as time went on I began to understand the expression, "Leslie Jensen and his thousand thieves". (Colonel Jensen, former governor of South Dakota, was another 147th FA officer). It was universally agreed that the showers were absolutely the best features of our camp. The sun and tropic temperature had the water 'just right', and during daylight it wasn't even necessary to use a towel. Of course, the 'baths' were out in the open, no women near, and Australia's native aborigines (who didn't often bathe) steered clear of those "crazy, white, splashing things".

On January 16 we had a big celebration involving both the 147th and 148th Battalions. The event was a flag raising ceremony, complete with drills, speeches and band music. This marked the first time that an American flag was raised on Australian soil. It was also noted that we, the 147th and 148th, were the first American Expeditionary Force of World War II and had made the longest troop movement in history, 9,000 miles and 6 weeks on the sea. We were also the first, and probably the only Americans to be part of the Australian Army.

Darwin is located on a peninsula where low hills or cliffs slope to the sea, no real beaches except near the harbor itself. Otherwise the surrounding terrain is mostly flat and barely above sea level at high tide. The harbor here is noteworthy for the extremely high (30' or more) rise and fall of tides. The area where most of our time was spent was in the wooded and brushy 'jungle' where tall eucalyptus trees predominated. There were patches of tall grasses mixed with smaller shrubs extend-

An Unexpected Journey

ing into the wooded areas, in a zone where the grassy plains sort of merged with the jungle. This is the typical "bush" or "outback" of the Aussie's description and, more specifically in this northern part of the country, is known as the Aborigine's "never-never land". Along most of the coastlines are mangrove trees where their roots usually extend into the high tide surf. The mangroves also are found inland in rivers, swamps and deep waterholes called "billabongs" in Aboriginal and Australian lingo.

Crossing these mangrove thickets is a nerve-shattering experience, due to the maze of interlocking roots that hide just below the surface of the muddy soup in which the trees grow. In addition, the nature of growth results in plants of 15' height with a thick umbrella-like spread at the top. Thus in a swamp, little sunlight reaches the water or mud so that a twilight atmosphere results at midday. A step into such an environment usually results in your foot being caught in roots that you cannot see. Needing to cross a 200' to 1000' stretch of this thicket with a weapon and pack can severely try ones mettle.

Because of its proximity to the equator, temperatures are high, 100 degrees F and higher in the daytime are common. The rainy season, Australia's "wet", usually extends at least through January and March when up to 90 inches of rainfall is expected. You can guess what the humidity is like. Naturally there is an abundance of insects and reptiles, including 4' long lizards and 10' long boa constrictors. Crocodiles are plentiful in both the harbor and in inland water holes. Water buffalo tend to hide out in wooded areas near rivers and swamps, while kangaroos can often be seen literally 'flying' through the air in those localities where the grass reaches heights of 6' to 8'. The soil throughout this area must be seen to be believed; it is uniformly red. In the 'wet' season it is mud and for the rest of the year becomes a fine powdery dust if disturbed.

Darwin town was a scene out of a century ago, reminding me of the dusty, brawling Wild West towns of America's 1800's lawless settlements. It was originally a penal colony, where non-violent convicts could opt to go and work for wages instead of serving their sentences in the more pleasant climate prisons in the south. The work was primarily loading and unloading ships at Darwin's jetties. Many Asiatics, Orientals and Negroes eventually arrived, many being of unsavory tendencies. There were, of course, many drunken brawls, fights and robberies, so few of our troops ventured there, although at first we were not officially forbidden to go. One trip to this inhospitable place was enough for me. Some of the Australian troops, having been stationed here for a long time, found it was great sport to frequent the many gambling dens and bars. Due to the frequent fights, muggings, etc., the town was eventually declared 'off limits'.

On February 19, 1942, less than three months after celebrating on Waikiki beaches came the dreaded Japanese attack on Australia. (They had finally caught up with us!) It was eventually learned that this first raid was conducted by the same commander and squadrons that had destroyed the American bases at Guam and Hawaii. We were taken by surprise when a fleet of very high-flying aircraft, coming from the south passed over. It was at first assumed this would be the American support promised by U.S. President Roosevelt after the fall of Manila and Singapore, and most of the troops, American and Australian alike, stood out in the open looking

An Ulvog Journey

up. Then suddenly the airplanes, in U-turns and treetop levels came roaring back, bombing and strafing everything in sight. It was a very rude awakening to say the least. I am not sure about the number of planes, it appeared to be a virtual swarm, but a count by Australian anti-aircraft gunners near the harbor put it at 64 heavy (4-motored) bombers, 71 dive bombers, 180 fighters (Zeros) and several which appeared to be primarily observation craft. Some radio broadcasts reported 400 airplanes total. The noise of the motors alone, at such a low elevation, was deafening and adding to that was the sound of bombs bursting and the chatter of machine guns. I was thankful for the foxhole/slit trench I had prepared. The destruction all around was horrendous, especially at the harbor and the town site. For about a week we were bombed and strafed every day at noon, but by gradually fewer planes. It seemed to be pointless, since the first raid pretty well wiped out the town, ruined the jetties, blew up the oil and gasoline tanks nearby, sank 8 large ships and badly damaged 14 others (including a hospital ship which had just entered the harbor) and shot down the Australian and American planes which had managed to get airborne, plus destroying those on the ground. Because the 147th was out in the 'bush' we were not a prime target, (well hidden) so although badly shaken and initially "shell shocked" were not hurt at first. Many Aussies, however, were wounded and some killed, mainly because of exposed locations, such as anti-aircraft gun batteries.

If there had been any sympathy for the Japanese before the raids, it vanished when we observed Aussie and American pilots being strafed in midair after parachuting from their disabled planes, or while crawling away from a crash. Both the hospital near town and the hospital ship were painted white with large red crosses on sides and top, yet they were bombed and strafed repeatedly.

As soon as it became apparent that this fierce 'storm' had subsided, Darwin, what was left of it, became a ghost town. A stream of frightened, dirty, near-exhausted refugees, most without belongings, poured out of there making a hasty retreat down the only road south. Some came in overcrowded cars and trucks, a few on horseback, more on bicycles, but most were afoot and practically all in panic, all jostling or shoving each other in their haste. I do not know what eventually became of them, for the next town or settlement to the south was over 70 miles away.

Between and during the successive attacks on the Darwin area the military was busily engaged in many 'un-militaristic' activities, repairing buildings such as the hospital and airplane hangers and shops, salvaging food, ammunition, gasoline, etc., burying the dead, helping injured, roaming through the jungle with Aussie and Aboriginal guides to rescue soldiers and sailors who had escaped from sinking and burning ships, and serving as perimeter guards. There was great fear of invasion by sea, paratroop landings behind our so-called 'lines', and sabotage by resident aliens or former criminal dockworkers.

In a 'search and rescue' party I learned to have great respect for the wisdom of our Aboriginal guide. He did not speak much but did a lot of humming and muttering as we made our way through the grass and bushes. It seemed as if our progress was slow and erratic for he inspected many leaves, twigs and blades of grass and this obviously influenced our constantly changing direction. Some of us "educated" folks considered abandoning this apparent 'fumbling' around, but then realized we

An Unexpected Journey

were thoroughly lost. Amazingly, we came upon a badly burned, cut, and dehydrated sailor who was nearly delirious. We half walked and half carried him out and were again amazed that we emerged from the jungle at the same spot we had entered. No wonder that these black "children of nature" are famous for their tracking ability.

One of the more fascinating undertakings that I was involved with at this time was salvaging. It was obvious that the 'would be invaders' knew of our every move, else how could they have known that Darwin's harbor was literally full of ships awaiting unloading, several of which arrived the evening before the raid, the hospital ship loaded with casualties from Timor and other East Indies fighting had barely dropped anchor that very morning. A tanker had just that morning tied up at the jetty and was unloading its fuel oil through a pipeline that went right up a hill to storage tanks. One of the first bombs went straight down the tanker's funnel, blowing up the ship, the jetty and the pipeline, acting as a fuse carried fire to the tank battery. The timing was incredible.

One or more of the sunken ships carried supplies for us Americans, ammunition, clothing, food, etc., the first support for our long lost, and we thought abandoned expeditionary force. As mentioned, the Japanese' first and subsequent raids came at midday, which coincided with high tide. At night when the tide was low, the sunken ships were almost fully exposed and trucks could be driven to or near them. Large holes were cut with acetylene torches in ship's sides and we removed large quantities of canned foods, ammunition, gasoline in 55 gallon barrels, and clothing. This was done at night because of low tide, of course, and also to avoid possible detection by enemy planes. I remember particularly the canned foods, as many labels had come unglued because of the seawater soaking, and opening the can was the only way to know the contents. Since we had no refrigeration the cooks devised some unusual meals, but I for one really appreciated the pineapple and other tropical fruit. We had not seen fruit, other than dried, for a month.

By now us Americans had been quite well assimilated into the Australian life style, manners, language, etc., and it was difficult to distinguish between an Aussie and a Yank. We ate the same food, spoke pretty much the same lingo, were paid in the same kind of money, and we even modified our clothing to resemble theirs, i.e., cut off the shirt sleeves and trouser legs. A backpack became "me swag", truck became "lorry", insects, reptiles and disliked officers were "buggers" and the universally used curse or swear word was "bloody". The 147th thus was often referred to by both Aussies and Yanks as the "bloody one four seven bloody guns" when profanity was called for. Any civilian was a "bloke" and most of those who appeared unkempt or hostile were considered "wharfies" whether or not they were dock laborers.

In the confusion and near chaos following the initial daily raids, much looting of the destroyed or damaged buildings went on, not only by any civilians remaining in the area but also by Aussie and Yank troops. On one such foray I went along, but was too disgusted or nauseated by the sights and smells to be an effective collector. I did pick up several phonograph records from an assorted jumble of books, magazines and bric-a-brac, after seeing another man from my battery carrying a portable hand-cranked phonograph. Although I wouldn't have given much for

An Ulvog Journey

the chance that the phonograph might be operable, my contribution (records) to the cause (music) seemed worthwhile, i.e., carrying back to camp. The beat up, partly scorched phonograph did work and got a good amount of it too, I only remember one of the recorded songs I had salvaged, "The Woodpecker Song".

To restore order the Darwin area was declared to be under full military control and a "Town Major" was appointed. Only the Australian Military Police were allowed to be within the town site and, with their authorization, those workers in reconstruction or repair of facilities such as the hospital and jetties. When officials from military units wished to search for useable and needed articles or materials amongst the debris of the town, the Town Major would grant a "chit", license to loot, and presumably keep records of the goods taken. Thus the salvaging or looting continued although on an orderly and controlled basis. Someone in the 147th came upon a large commercial-type cement mixer on wheels in a wrecked building and, after dragging away building wreckage with the truck, pulled the mixer loose and back to camp. From then on the 147th showers had concrete floors and, after sometime, we also had concrete floors in our tents. We moved to other locations, much to our protests, but the cement mixer on steel wheels, towed by its rescue truck and followed by truck loads of looted pipe and barrels gave our convoy the appearance of a gypsy caravan.

On March 17th we were surprised in a visit by General MacArthur who was escaping from the Philippines. This was undoubtedly the least formal and most unpicturesque appearance he ever made. Maybe he even forbid photographs since his appearance and demeanor was in sharp contrast to all news items and pictures I've ever seen. Of course, there were no newspaper reporters present, only dusty, dirty, sweaty half-naked Yanks and Aussies. His visit was short while he demanded quick transportation to Melbourne, about as far from Darwin as he could get in Australia. On March 20th he made his "I shall return" speech in Adelaide. At about this time the entire Northern Province of Australia was placed under full military control due to the devastating Darwin raids, as well as the Japanese capture of Singapore and Manila.

March 30th saw us being bombed and strafed for the first time in the middle of the night. This pretty well confirmed the beliefs of all the military commanders that Australia was about to be invaded and the Darwin harbor vicinity was the logical entry point. Consequently, all of the Australian, American and British army personnel were ordered to prepare for it. At that time there was no prospect of reinforcements. There were a few short roads, mostly narrow, winding dirt trails in the immediate vicinity of Darwin town site, but only one fairly straight graded road, also dirt, leading south. Because of jungle, treacherous creeks and 'billabongs' it was assumed the invaders would follow the main road. So the strategy was to pull the main forces back away from the town site proper and dig in and fortify positions on both sides of the road, whereby the advancing enemy would be caught in cross fires. Our guns, howitzers, machine guns, mortars, etc., were dug down to near barrel height and barricaded with logs and packed dirt. Fire lanes, oriented to intersect the road at various distances, were prepared by cutting down grass, brush and trees. Anyone who has not cut down a mature Northern Australian eucalyptus tree cannot comprehend the frus-

An Unexpected Journey

trating labor this requires. They are 40' to 50' tall, have few branches except at and near the top, are 7" to 10" diameter at the base, and hard. It was common for axes to glance or bounce off the trunk and for the trunk to ring as if it was a steel pipe. We cut down dozens of these trees for fire lanes, using them for breastworks. Of course, that meant cutting logs several times. As an added attraction to this logging 'fun', some of the trees had a small hollow center occupied by ants, the bites of which generally drew blood. In small clearings and open grassy areas these ants built huge rock-hard mounds or pillars where apparently a tree had provided the base or starting point. Another kind of ant mound was more common in open sunny areas, built by insects which must have had a built-in compass since their tall, thin, narrow mounds were oriented in a north-south direction. Both types of mounds commonly reached eight feet in height and had skeletal remains of birds and mouse-size animals near the base. Australian police who worked with the natives (Aborigines) cautioned us not to sit close to these anthills for their shade and/or back support, as human skeletons had been found resting against them.

With our guns now prepared for direct fire there was little need for conventional artillery fire-direction crews, and being a member of such, I had been assigned to the newly formed Perimeter Defense group. Thus I had many opportunities for investigating these strange and remarkable constructions. I also made a concerted search, not only for likely infiltrators, but also for possible edible fruit, plants or roots, and together with others who had looked, decided there was nothing to suit our tastes. The native black "nature's children" had been living off this land for thousands of years but we eventually learned their diets were various kinds of insects, grubs from dead or dying trees, rats or gophers, occasional wallabies (killed with boomerangs or spears), snakes, lizards and the like, all eaten raw, of course. Declining such fare we instead went hunting for kangaroo or water buffalo meat and were quite successful, especially with respect to the latter. However, cornering either of these big animals can be hazardous to one's health.

Practically all of the foods we were supplied came in powdered or dehydrated form. The 147th cooks did the best they could, and one of their best products was bread, which was served at almost every meal. The only complaint was, due to the daytime heat, bread was made at night by the light of gasoline lanterns. The result was dough in which a goodly supply of flying insects became embedded. Initially we Yanks would hold a slice of bread against the sunlight and pick out the black inclusions but, noticing no such actions by the Aussies, we were soon taking the bread straight, 'crunchies' and all. After the first revulsions (mental) were overcome, most of us declared that the bread was indeed good. Undoubtedly we were, as the Aussie's put it, fair dinkum troppo, i.e., well along to being mentally affected by the tropics.

On April 4th another Japanese raid took us by surprise. Possibly we had become a bit lax in preparedness due to the relative ineffectiveness of recent flyovers. This time a few of the 147th fellows out of their trenches or foxholes caught some bomb fragments but were not seriously wounded. The Japanese were now using a new type of bomb called a "daisy cutter", which although not large, had an extended detonation rod that caused the explosion to occur about 3' above ground level and spread small fragments in a horizontal circular pattern. These anti-personnel devices

An Ulvog Journey

were dropped in clusters or scattered close together. Several troops were caught in a standing or running position and were nearly cut in half by these "daisy cutters".

A most memorable day is April 14th when the mail came. This was when we first had mail from America since leaving California. Most of this was Christmas cards, but there were also a few newspapers. It was from these papers that we learned that "the 147th Field Artillery was missing at Pearl Harbor, presumably sunk". I do not know when our letters from Darwin reached home, but later mail brought newspaper accounts of memorial services for us. I suppose we "bloody one four seven" guys could claim another 'first' reading about our own funerals?

At about this time, it was being reported in radio broadcasts and in newspapers that Australia was in imminent danger of invasion, so it was no surprise that war correspondents began arriving in the vicinity of Darwin. The American reporters stayed with the 147th and sent out some startling and vivid news dispatches regarding conditions.

On April 25th and 27th we were again visited by some of the Japanese air force, resulting in two 147th officers killed and their Jeep driver seriously wounded. They were going down the road and didn't hear or see the Japanese planes until too late. The officers jumped from the still moving vehicle and were running for cover and the driver had stopped but had not completely disembarked when the bomb exploded. Presumably the Jeep caught most of the fragments which would have killed the driver had he been a little faster in getting away from it.

Although there was general concern that the invasion was due, the commander of the 147th, Colonel Scurr, decided it was probably unlikely, due to the problems the Japanese would have supplying an occupation force here. His arguments convinced the war correspondents and they soon departed. In the meantime the Australian armed forces had been reinforced so the need for our presence diminished.

Everything changed about the first of June when a large convoy of Japanese ships was spotted coming in our direction and we were alerted. On June 4th, the remnants of the U.S. Navy (which was largely destroyed at Pearl Harbor six months previously) engaged the Japanese fleet in what became known as the battle of the Coral Sea or the battle of Midway. Many books have been written about this engagement, all of which refer to it as the "turning point of the war". It certainly proved to be a turning point for the South Dakota 147th and 148th Field Artillery.

Seven months after our brief 'frolic' at Waikiki we were leaving the God-forsaken outpost of North Australia. On June 29th we packed and loaded our trucks for another 'first'. A convoy, including a large number of men, proceeded down a dirt trail, described as "one lane wide and four lanes deep in dust", leading through the middle of Australia and the Great Stony Desert. Books have been written about the trials and tribulations of this historic journey. It seemed as if we spent months on the move, stopping at night when the cooks prepared the evening meal and next morning's breakfast. We camped out (theoretically) on folding cots, but many, including myself, preferred to rest in the trucks. I don't recall anyone undressing for bed once we reached the desert--blistering hot days and freezing nights.

An Unexpected Journey

CHAPTER SIX
Return to Civilization

On July 8th we arrived at Ballarat in the Australian province of Victoria, after 9 days of a spectacular but often nightmarish journey. If any of our 147th dirty, unkempt refugees failed to become adopted by someone in the throng that met our arrival it would have been their own fault. One of my buddies, Bill Ross, and I accepted the invitation to accompany a little "Limey" type Aussie to his home for baths and supper. We were treated royally, enjoyed the three small children, answered a multitude of questions by both the man and his gracious wife, and promised to return for a visit as soon as we were settled in camp and permitted to leave there. It was wintertime "down under" and was quite cold and rainy. The city literally gave us a beautiful park, in which were botanical gardens and a pond with various waterfowl, including swans. There was a building with showers, toilets and a boiler room and furnace, which may have been installed as an attraction to bring us there. Our tents were arranged in rows as near as possible to this building, although the area was in the lowest part of the park. As a result our camp location eventually became a literal swamp.

Thus it was not long before Bill Ross and I were visitors at the Arch and Phylis Nicols home where we had been invited. It seems that, especially in the south of Australia, the Northern Territory was practically unknown until the Japanese raids brought attention to it. So it was, when the people here in the 'civilized' established South heard that the U. S. troops were defending Darwin, their gratitude was overwhelming. We were literally taken in as family members.
The Nicols children, with whom I still correspond, address me as "big brother". Their other adopted "brother" was later killed in action and it fell to me the job of telling and consoling them.

By this time we had lost quite a few men, mostly to the tropical diseases, malaria, dengue, 'jungle rot', etc., and slow-healing wounds. Replacements, mostly draftees, were sent to fill our ranks, and new equipment, most of which we had never before seen, also appeared. Up to now our weapons and clothes were World War I leftovers. The old French 75 mm howitzers were swapped for new 105 mm guns; the old Springfield and Enfield rifles were replaced by the Garand, etc. Before long the old 147th of just 8 months previous did not look much like the reorganized regiment. And even the new recruits discovered there were a few things that the old 'salts' could teach them.

Since we were now in open country, farms and meadows, the 147th began again to be 'field' artillery. Consequently there were many drills and practice runs with which to become familiar as well as actual firing maneuvers.

After the 26-hour days and 8-day weeks that we had become used to during the 'Darwin Despair', it seemed as if our reward was a good amount of free time. Weekends, often of 3 days duration, and weeklong furloughs were common. Many men discovered the city of Melbourne, about 60 miles to the south. It was a common occurrence to see groups of 5 or 6 men, each leaving the Ballarat camp in char-

An Ulvog Journey

coal-powered taxicabs Friday afternoon, returning early Monday morning. I made several such journeys and enjoyed them, although I tried to go on a 3-day pass so as to get at least 4 days in the big city. Transportation in those times of strict petrol (gasoline) rationing was, as the Aussies said, "a bit dear", (expensive).

On September 24th I was "volunteered" as a pallbearer for a Battery F man who had been ill in the hospital and died there. (The Army system: "I want four volunteers, you, you, you and you"). Actually, I think this fellow's health problem began, or was aggravated, with alcohol; bad rum when at Darwin and too much good gin at Ballarat. The three-month stay at Ballarat was undoubtedly the bright spot of our entire overseas sojourn. Several 147th men were married there. Others, who were trying to catch up on their thirst after the dry, dusty, hot Darwin days, spent much of their off-duty time at the Ballarat Brewery guest lounge (free suds for all yanks!). My adopted 'father', Arch Nicol was employed there, but neither he nor I were' beer addicts. Rather our outings were visits to gold mines and greyhound races. Regretfully it came time to leave the pleasant camp and town.

CHAPTER SEVEN
Leaving a Second Home

So on October 7th we again loaded up and headed north. Our new 'digs', reached 5 days later, was about 30 or 40 miles from Brisbane, Queensland, and out in the jungle. This was known as Camp Cable, a miserably wet and cold wooded area, where the 147th had been assigned to I Corps. The 32nd Division was also at this camp and part of I Corps. The 32nd was the mobilized Wisconsin National Guard, which had served along with the 147th in World War I. Obviously somewhere along the way the 147th and 148th had ceased to be part of the Australian Army and was back in the U.S. Armed Forces. I do not know when it happened, but suspect it was while we were at Ballarat. Things would never be the same again.

After training with the 32nd for a time, we were ordered to a new camp much closer to Brisbane, I do not know the official date because it seemed to be a gradual irregular change of location, nor do I know the official name of the new camp; however, it was generally and irreverently known as Camp Swampy. It was almost a repeat of our Darwin camps, except now it was cold and wet. Once established here we were given short one-day passes to town and provided transportation also, because time off in camp was miserable. In town I became acquainted with a man, Len, and his wife, Chick, who were motorcyclists, each having their own cycles. Sometimes one of them, usually the lady, would loan a cycle to me so that I could ride along the coast or into the countryside. At other times a sidecar would be attached to one of the machines so all three of us could tour. One of these tours led to a pineapple plantation, or farm, the owner of which was well known. There he showed us how to select a fully ripened pineapple and invited us to pick some from the field. This we did and proceeded to eat ripe, fresh pineapple right there. I will never forget this tour, my hosts, or the taste of fresh, field ripened pineapple. I failed to note the date, unfortunately, but it would have been near Christmas, 1942. Possibly it was on Christmas.

An Unexpected Journey

There was another very memorable event relating to Camp Swampy, again undated other than late December or early January 1943. A group, of which I was one, had passes for Brisbane with transportation provided. I cannot recall what our activities were in town but three of us managed to get lost and were late reaching the agreed 'pick up' or assembly point for the return ride to camp. Although camp was 15 miles or so distant and it was night, there seemed to be no alternative to walking, which we began to do. Before going very far, a local farmer or rancher in an ancient flatbed truck came along and stopped, offering us a ride. "Hop on boys, I'll drop you at the road to your bloody mud hole". We did hop onto the flat bed and as the truck gained speed, discovered that the boards of the bed had worn out over the rear wheels, thus giving us a mud shower bath. Yet when he stopped at a road intersection and wished us a "cheerio, chin up cobbers" goodnight, we thanked him in spite of the muddy ride, for we were about three-fourths of the way to camp. By now the light drizzle had turned to rain and we resumed walking on or alongside the muddy road. Occasionally a vehicle heading towards camp passed us by, ignoring our waving and shouting.

One of the trio, not I, became furious after failing to halt several such vehicles and engaged the others in his plan to stop the very next one, if there were any, coming down the road. When the lights of a vehicle triggered the plan, we removed our ponchos and stood in the roadway waving wildly. A command car stopped, a rear door opened, and a voice calmly called, "Hop in boys". Upon the question, "What battery?", we all said "F". The fellow who instigated the stop had developed such a foul attitude that he continued to curse the rain, the mud, being passed by, the army, our campsite and the world in general. Suddenly I noticed a glint of light reflected from the shoulders of the man in the front passenger seat and began prodding the haranguer (elbow to ribs fashion) while pointing to the obvious insignia. Instead of silencing him, he turned on me with "Cut it out, why are you poking me?" The command car stopped at the Battery F tent row where an overhead light revealed the insignia to be eagles. Colonel Scurr turned and said, "Here you are boys, have a good night." No threats, no questions and, as it turned out, no reports and no brig or demotions. Many years later Kenneth Scurr attended a 147th Battery reunion in Vermillion, South Dakota. Upon my asking if he remembered such an event, he looked at me rather strangely and said, "How did you know about that?" When I explained that I was one of the "Musketeers", he slapped my back, bought us drinks and said, "That's what I always liked about my South Dakota boys, guts!"

So it is, that while most of the 147th, the 32nd and I Corps men had nothing but bad memories of the Brisbane area, I have some shining good ones. Oh yes, although not exactly a memory of Camp Swampy or Camp Cable, there is a pleasant memory related thereto. In mid-December I was granted a furlough (one week or so) to go back to Melbourne and Ballarat, visiting there with the friends who had welcomed me so grandly when I came, literally as a refugee from Darwin. It was a big morale booster and turned out to be really 'just what the doctor ordered', because three days after returning to my battery, I was once more 'volunteered' as a casket bearer. One funeral was for a 147th F Battery man and another on the same day for a Merchant Marine.

An Ulvog Journey

During the training as a field artillery unit at Camp Cable and Swampy, the 147th acquired a small Piper 4 cylinder airplane nicknamed "Grasshopper". This was an expansion of our Fire Direction (Instrument) Center, which had been almost eliminated in Darwin's operation. Up to now, cooperation with the Army and Navy for aerial observation had proved to be very helpful, so we would now have airborne observers as well. It should be mentioned that in the 1940's there was no U.S. Air Force per se, military aircraft being from either the U.S. Army or U.S. Navy. The little Piper plane, designated L-4 (Liaison 4-cylinder) was a small, highly maneuverable but slow craft, as we would say derogatorily, "100 mph at full throttle with a strong tail wind". Later a second L-4 was assigned to the 147th when aerial observation proved valuable.

CHAPTER EIGHT
Northward Bound

It was time to leave the Brisbane area, so on February 20th the 147th again loaded up and headed north. Our new camp was not far from Rockhampton, Queensland, where our convoy arrived after three days travel and three nights of bivouacking. I have few memories of the Rockhampton town or the nearby camp. There seemed to be much confusion, although our battery was busy at simulated battle conditions, including howitzer firing. Apparently the 148th Field Artillery had become separated from us and even the two 147th battalions were being divided. I eventually learned that First Battalion was re-designated as 260th Field Artillery and the original Second Battalion of the 147th became First Battalion, which included changing our battery designations to A, B and C. During the five months based at Rockhampton, both the 147th battalions and the 148th were involved in expeditions to various islands in the Coral Sea area, but in most cases by relatively small parties.

A rather large force, in which I participated, attacked Kiriwina, one of the Trobriand Islands, in the Solomon Sea. It was very lightly defended by the Japanese and the 147th soon returned to Australia. One of the islands that the Japanese had taken, New Britain, was also relatively near Australia, as well as a block to the U.S. drive toward the Philippines. From aerial observations and reports by Australian Coast Watchers in the Soloman Islands and elsewhere, it had been determined that the main town of Rabaul in New Britain, together with its seaport, was heavily fortified. Actually this had been confirmed by an attempted landing by either Australian or American forces or both. The strategy developed for capturing the island involved a 'back-door' approach whereby a small, armed group would land from the sea in morning darkness on the presumably uninhabited shore on the opposite from Rabaul. This group would only stay long enough for the Japanese occupation forces to be distracted, at which time the main U.S. force would take the city and port, I was one of the "hit and run" group, presumably in case artillery fire would be needed once we were established and our escape cut off. This operating technique was employed at other strategic points with great success, but not in this case. First our maps were ancient and unreliable. The proposed landing site was not a beach as assumed, but a narrow strip of rocky shore backed by an almost vertical 10' to 15' high cliff with

An Unexpected Journey

roots protruding and dense jungle at the top. Secondly, the supposedly calm, clear bay was full of coral reefs, which could cut the bottoms out of our landing boats (LCI - Landing Craft Infantry). The result was that no boat reached land; all personnel waded and stumbled through several hundred feet of irregular ocean floor to reach shore.

After no more than half of our group had climbed to the top of the cliff, the Japs opened fire with rifles, grenades and mortars. The landing boats had stopped offshore as soon as they hit coral pinnacles and were anchored there. The resulting hasty retreat back to the boats was in a shower of bullets and grenades. Oddly, but fortunately, no boat was seriously damaged and no one was killed or badly wounded. After rethinking the nightmare of this 'evacuation' I marvel at the fact that not one person was left on that miserable island. Incidentally, neither the U.S. nor Australia took Rabaul despite numerous attempts. It was finally cut off and the Japanese were starved out.

As if to add injury to insult, i.e., the insult of retreat, I was with a different group of the 147th to make a landing at Japen Island, in the Geelvink Bay area of northwestern Dutch Guinea, or so I heard. Actually, I never saw the island. The operating method, which became more or less standard, involved rapid transport through dangerous waters via a converted destroyer ship (APD) to near the target area, there to transfer the troops to small LCI's for shore landing. Embarking on and debarking from a destroyer type ship on the sea involved the use of landing nets, sort of 10' to 15' wide rope ladders tied to the ship's deck railing. In unloading quickly from a ship on the water, one simply reached over the railing, grasped the landing net, somersaulted over the rail, climbed down the net to near the level of the landing boat and, with care, jumped into the small boat. While both watercraft had stopped horizontal movement, action of the water caused vertical rocking and rolling. Consequently, the smaller boat often bumped into the larger and sometimes moved some distance from it; hence one did not merely step off the ladder into the landing craft. This time I happened to be standing on the destroyer deck near where a landing net was being tied in preparation for our debarking, and when the order came, I grabbed the net at the end where it was supposedly tied. The last memory I had of this entire 'invasion' was the somersault. When I regained consciousness in the 5th General Hospital in Rockhampton, I was told that the net had come loose or slipped, whereupon my handhold failed and I made a belly-flop landing on the LCI's steel floor some 15' below. I do not know exactly when this flying leap occurred, except it was in the early morning darkness of March 1943. Three months of 'imprisonment' in a plaster and iron cast, enclosing at least three fourths of my body, is my main recollection of the Rockhampton experience. When the cast was finally cut and broken away, I could not arise unaided nor stand alone, but had a walking cast on the broken leg and an adjustable aluminum cast or brace on my broken arm. After a few days of physical therapy, when could take care of myself, I was offered a one-month "convalescent furlough".

Although I couldn't go back to the 147th or home, the hospital administrators wanted to get patients out and on their own as quickly as possible to make room for daily incoming casualties. So, while not forcing anyone out, the restricted furlough did entice many, including myself, to leave. The provisions, other than no return home or to combat, were check-ins at American or Australian military facilities at periodic intervals (preferably daily), advise attendants there of changes in your itinerary, if any, and return to Fifth General Hospital at the prescribed time. Since travel on a furlough required finances, and a soldier could only receive his service pay from his company, there was an arrangement whereby 'chits' for partial pay advances could be used. As mentioned, I had made acquaintances at Ballarat, Melbourne, Sydney and Brisbane, plus I had corresponded with relatives and friends of Aussies with whom we served at Darwin, at their request, and thus had contacts with folks in many places. Obviously, I looked up and visited many of these people with the result that I spent only one or two nights at hotels in the entire month of "gadding about" in south and east Australia.

One acquaintance in Sydney who was to play a significant role in my life, Joyce Bullock, took great pains to insure that this visit here and later would be most memorable.

CHAPTER NINE
A Taste of New Guinea

In early July, after discharge from the hospital, I was once again with the 147th Battery F. On July 26th we sailed from Rockhampton and reached Milne Bay at the southeastern shore of New Guinea, the following evening. Although it was generally known that the 148th had preceded us, but also that the Japanese had invaded the island, it was a tense nervous group that went ashore that evening, myself included. We had just been issued some new jungle gear that we had not used before. The one outstanding item, in my memory, was the jungle hammock. I'm sure whoever invented the thing made a nice fortune promoting it to the War Department, but had no concept of the terrain, climate or other conditions facing us. It was dark and raining when we were ordered to scatter into the jungle nearby and put up for the night. The ground was soggy everywhere. According to a brief lecture and demonstration aboard ship, preceding the issuance of the new gear, we should tie the hammock to trees and keep it as high above the grass and brush as possible, but still be able to get into it. This 'thing' was really an ingenious contraption, actually a one-piece screened bed with an overhead canopy and zippered entryway on one side. I found two coconut trees the proper distance apart, trampled down the undergrowth, tied up the hammock and crawled in. Of course, in situations like this we remained fully dressed, day and night, ready to go at a moment's notice. Most of us also kept our rifle or pistol in bed with us, or at least had our bayonet handy. Another new item issued us was a "black-out light". It was a one-cell flashlight, mostly non-metallic, with a lens that focused a thin beam of rather dull illumination. Plastics, as they are known now, had not yet been developed. Henry Ford had been experimenting with something made from soybeans and had used it for steering wheels, crank handles on window lifts, door lock knobs, etc., on some cars, so we nicknamed our synthetic flashlights 'Fords'.

Night in the jungle is not quiet, but a really tired person can usually get

An Unexpected Journey

some rest, and I was soon sound asleep. After a bit I was aroused and tried to sit up but bumped my head. Next I tried, but failed, to open one of the zippers in the screened side of the hammock. Near panic, I found the second zipper and managed to open it enough to crawl out. As I stood up, I saw what appeared to be the green eyes of an animal about 10' away. After observing this for a moment I shone the 'Ford' light on the spot. Nothing was there except the usual underbrush. Then in the darkness I saw more of the green spots; again with the light - nothing. The whole weird experience was my introduction to the phosphorescence of decaying jungle plants in a water-soaked environment. Next I investigated what had happened to my carefully installed hammock. While I slept, the coconut trees leaned, roots and all, toward each other until the sagging hammock reached the ground. One of them leaned so far that it was resting partly on the canopy so that when I rared up half awake the tree trunk whacked my skull. When the hammock sagged to the ground the screened sides were pulled out of shape, causing the zippers to jam. It was obvious that if I wanted any more sleep that night some rearranging was in order. So I just untied the hammock, which then collapsed, slid it away from the leaning trees and laid down on top. In the commotion, several of my compadres were aroused and had similar or comparable nightmarish trials. At least one buddy slashed wildly with his bayonet to speed his eviction from the screen and canvas 'trap'. In the morning I very carefully folded and packed my GI (government issue) hammock, but there were more than a few of those things left where they lay, so-called "lost in combat". Some time later we could all laugh and joke about our first New Guinea night, but I, for one, will never forget it.

There was for me mostly confusion and miserable living here in Papua, New Guinea. There were detail duties besides artillery drills. One of the detail assignments that came my way involved crossing Milne Bay by a water-going land vehicle designated DUKW, nicknamed "duck" by most servicemen. I do not recall what sort of supplies were needed from the south side of the bay nor the date of the trip but, before it was finished, I had vowed to never cross any sizeable waterway in such a machine again. Our group included probably six or seven men in addition to the driver. Going over was a nice morning cruise on a relatively calm ocean. Coming back with two less crewmembers but with many crates of supplies, the 'duck' rode very low in the water, averaging about two inches of open hold above the water line, so that waves occasionally splashed over. At less than one-half of the way across, the water became quite rough (storm approaching) with large waves cutting clear over the sides. This truck-boat rig is slow on either land or water but it now appeared as if it stalled or shifted into reverse as I looked towards the north shore. It was the longest and scariest water cruise I've been on. Why we didn't sink I'll never know.

On or about August 1, 1943, the 147th prepared to make a ship landing at a point farther north along the northeast New Guinea coast. I did not feel well but boarded the ship anyway. A medic came and told me he needed to check on my physical condition, because of the recent hospitalization. His diagnosis was I was in the initial stage of malaria. Back to the Fifth General Hospital I went, and was shortly experiencing violent illness. I don't know how long it lasted because part of the time I was only about half conscious, but it was a month or so before I began to think I might survive. When my hospital discharge was pending, probably in September, it

An Ulvog Journey

was determined that the 147th FA was at Oro Bay, about 200 miles from Milne Bay and also on the northeast coast of New Guinea.

Communication and transportation problems at this time were severe and there was much confusion, at least among the enlisted personnel and lower ranked commissioned officers. So it should have been no surprise to learn, once I arrived at Oro Bay that my Battery F of the 147th was no longer there but was supposedly in the Finschhafen area of New Guinea. Because of ongoing combat there I was returned to the hospital, where my presence was not wanted either. So the next move was to a Replacement Center, the location of which is a mystery to me yet, other than a jungle clearing, reportedly in northwestern New Guinea in the Hollandia area. Again I have no dates recorded but it would have been in October 1943, I believe.

It was obvious that this camp had been recently established and was in a locality where intense combat had taken place. There were many enlisted men here and few officers, so that a near-chaos atmosphere prevailed. After reveille and roll call, there was little to do for most until another roll call at evening mess time. Occasionally work details were called and put in charge of noncommissioned officers, such as me, of whom there were a few. These assignments were usually simple and of short duration, such as policing an area, ie., picking up trash, clearing away some underbrush or putting gravel in muddy spots. Whereas most of the men, recruits and draftees, tended to stay in their tents reading, playing cards, gambling, etc., I did not know anyone there and it seemed as if some were sent to their destinations daily and yet others arrived. So in the abundance of free time, I explored the nearby jungle and was amazed to see the Japanese wreckage and abandoned material. One item that stands out sharply in my memory was a German-built command car (Daimler) that appeared to be in very good condition. It was big with three rows of seats, large wheels with tires in front, plus duplicates in front fender mounts, and tank-type tracks at the rear. Just what I needed, I thought: I inspected this machine several times and drooled over it, even though it was obvious I could never 'loot' it and bring it home. What really bothered me was the implication that we were fighting an enemy being supported by Germany. My stay at the replacement center seemed to go on for months, but was probably a week or two. By then the 147th was reportedly at Madang, about 200 miles northwest of Finschhafen and also on the northeast New Guinea coast.

Later I learned that I was not the only apparently lost and forgotten Yank when Colonel Scurr's diary referred to the situation as follows:

Personnel replacements were seldom received in a timely manner. In one case it took nine months for forty-three replacements to reach us. This group arrived from the United States at Milne Bay in January, 1944. Several weeks earlier the 147th had left there to go to Woodlark and Kiriwina Islands. Because we were badly understaffed, an officer was sent to Milne Bay to get them. When he arrived the group had been sent to Oro Bay and then back to Australia. After the 147th had left Kiriwina the replacements were sent there. By then, April, we were at Finschhafen. By the time the wanderers got to Finschhafen the 147th was involved in the Wakde-Sarmi-Biak campaign. When this group arrived at Biak we had invaded Noemfoor. From Biak they were sent to Hollandia where

An Unexpected Journey

another officer finally found them and brought them to Noemfoor. Nine months' of mistakes.

I suspect I had crossed paths with this group, maybe more than once.

CHAPTER TEN
South Sea Cruise

There were U.S. boats at various ports and bays by now, possibly manned by the Coast Guard, and I, with four other servicemen from the Replacement Center, were hauled to the dock. We had been issued jungle rations for the expected three days of ocean travel, together with official identity and army unit documents. The patrol boats took us out in the bay, where we had been unable to see anything similar to military ships, and ultimately pulled alongside an ancient looking freighter, the "Von Spilbergen". After an exchange of some documents we were ushered aboard, scarcely believing what was happening. As the five of us standing on the deck were watching the boat which brought us speed back to shore, a ship's officer showed where we could take up our abode-just a rectangular space on the open steel deck. Shortly thereafter several dark-skinned Asiatics proceeded to stretch and tie up to some ship's riggings a canvas cover above our designated deck space. They apparently neither understood nor spoke English. We soon learned that we were aboard an old wooden Dutch freighter that had been covered with steel plates riveted and/or bolted to the hull. Even on the relatively calm Solomon Sea, that ancient tub creaked, squealed and groaned steadily. The crew was a mixture of Hindus, Moslems, Buddhists and possibly other East Asia religions, all dark-skinned, half-naked men. The officers who handled the ship and the crew were surely the proverbial "hard-headed Dutchmen". Though few, whenever they appeared on deck, they were dressed as if they had just stepped out of a fashion salon; gleaming white shirts, shining gold buttons and braid, and knife-edged creases in dark blue trousers. In ramrod-straight military bearing, the little they spoke was clear, brisk and short. They advised us against socializing with the crew and if we had trouble or were in need, to call on them in their cabins. We had hardly settled into our surroundings, beginning to enjoy the sailing when sudden loud, sharp voices were raised by two groups of crewmembers, apparently in disagreement about a deck task. We could only lay low and hope they didn't come any nearer to us, when, as if from nowhere, one of the ship's officers appeared in the midst of the squabbling groups and promptly stopped the commotion. Similar near riots broke out frequently and always an officer popped up in the middle of the group to restore order. At one time when the angry shouts were accompanied by upraised knives which seemed to have been grasped from midair, I could not restrain my admiration for anyone so fearless as to wade in and quell such a near uncontrollable group. Eventually I managed to catch an officer on deck, apparently on a routine inspection, and told him my feelings. He surprised me by smiling, acknowledged the compliment, and invited my companions and me to his cabin after his duty tour ended that evening. We found his quarters to be nicely furnished and he was relaxed in casual clothing and 'laid back'. He made his way to the ship's mess (kitchen) alone, and brought some drinks and snacks for us. This little deviation from

An Ulvog Journey

our otherwise boring existence, punctuated by occasional crew violence, was greatly appreciated, and was repeated by another officer. Under their outward appearance of stiff, brusque, and near mechanical demeanor, they were human and kind. I am not sure if I ever saw the ship's captain. We were only so much freight to him, contracted for through General MacArthur's Army. I suspect that the location of the 147th provided to the ship's captain by the replacement center officer may have been in error, or that my unit had moved on before we arrived there.

CHAPTER ELEVEN
Catching Up

After having made two port stops, locations unknown, we finally caught up with several army groups, one of which was the 147th. Planning was underway there, at Woodlark on Kulumadau in the Solomon Sea, for an invasion. Up until this time it seemed to me that there had been a great deal of confusion and illogical movements of various army units, in which many splits or temporary divisions occurred. For the average enlisted person it was impossible to understand it all. We were, of course, all in the United States Army commanded by General MacArthur at his Melbourne, Australia headquarters. Although it hadn't been obvious in our operations while we reorganized in southern Australia or even in the movements northward, it became clear that everything was being changed, especially after we left Australia. No more contacts with Australian troops, even though we operated in territory normally under Australia's rule. It just seemed as if MacArthur's taking command of the army began timidly and evolved into a dictatorial and maybe unreasonable style. From the notes and diary of a commissioned officer, I learned the following;

"The second battalion of the 147th FA moved to Milne Bay in late July 1943. The first battalion came also to Milne Bay in early August after its assignment with the Leatherback Force. Thus the 147th regiment was now together after a four month separation and was again under the command of Colonel Scurr."

By the time I reached the 147th, after the malaria bout, the battalions had been separated again and the second battalion was now attached to the 158th Infantry of the Arizona National Guard. This proved to be an exceptionally effective union and was ultimately named the 158th Regimental Combat Team (RCT). As it turned out, I was with this Team from then on.

On November 26, 1943 we landed at Kiriwina in the Trobriand Islands group without opposition. The Japanese had apparently bypassed this place, but raided it and bombed it a number of times. In the evening of December 20th, a weird raid by planes coming from different directions dropped 60 bombs (official count) on us without causing a great deal of property damage or many personnel injuries, but sleeping that night wasn't easy. Sometime toward the year's end Colonel Jensen visited his old 147th battalion for the last time. He was sent back to the U.S. suffering from malaria that finally ended his military career. On December 31, 1943, the second battalion of the 147th officially became the only 147th Field Artillery. Along with this reorganization, the first battalion became the 260th Field Artillery and its former battery designations assigned to the new 147th. Thus my old Battery

An Unexpected Journey

F became C, Battery E changed to B, and former Battery D was now A. Obviously the 147th was now just half of the size of the former 147th, and for this reason, and because it was now allied with the 158th Infantry in a combat team, became known as a "Baby Division". The new 260th actually ceased to be an artillery-firing unit, its howitzers went to a different group; I do not recall its name. Apparently the 148th Field Artillery was absorbed into some other division at either Ballarat or Brisbane, so I am not aware of our 147th being with them again.

    Kiriwina proved to be about as pleasant a place to be as anywhere away from Australia. Other than the occasional Japanese flyovers there was little to worry about, with the exception of tropical diseases. In February 1944 I did have a repeat run of dengue, apparently left over from an earlier, harder attack. Because our Medical Section was not now hard pressed to care for wounded or sick in hastily established facilities, they had set up a fairly good clinic, where I was cared for, thus avoiding shipment to a hospital (Australia?) then after recovery, on to another replacement center.

    While at Kiriwina, the medics made a study of the natives' health, since these Melanesians were quite friendly and cooperated with the doctors and assistants. The medics roamed over the island, together with an Australian official and a local tribal chief, visiting every village known. There they obtained blood samples for examination at their clinic and, after some double testing, concluded that 90% of the native population had malaria, most unknowingly. Apparently, after many generations living with the disease, they had developed a sort of immunity,

    In early April 1944 we moved to Finschhafen, where the 147th was reported to be when I was released from the hospital after my earlier malaria confinement. This is the only instance I know of that I was about six months ahead of my battery! This time, however, I did land at Finschhafen and with the proper unit. We set up camp inland from the docks in thick jungle. The rumor was that a fine pool for bathing, fed by a waterfall, was up in the mountains behind our camp, and the stream (river?) running by our camp would lead to this pool or pond. At the first opportunity four of us decided to investigate. We followed the stream up the mountainside, carrying towels and rifles. The farther we climbed the thicker was the undergrowth, as well as trees, but we did eventually find the waterfall and pool. While we rested and drew straws to determine the order in which we would bathe or swim, loud shouts and banging on trees and rocks above brought us up with rifles at ready. There was a group, ten or more, of black 'fuzzy-wuzzies' waving spears and clubs at us. No arguments from us as we backed away and then scrambled downhill to camp. Those guys didn't sound or act as if they intended to let us use their water hole. We found out later they were headhunters and cannibals of the highlands; too close for comfort!

    By now, there, was a great deal of support, men and materials, coming from the U.S., and General MacArthur was speeding up the advance toward the Philippines. After Finschhafen the 147th was often split up, with the two detachments assigned to different places. When we left Finschhafen after barely one month's stay, the 158th RCT was sent to Hollandia, Dutch New Guinea, 500 miles or more to the northwest. It seems this was intended as a brief stop, where part of the regiment went to Wakde Island and the part where I was, went to Sarmi. This came to be known as

An Ulvog Journey

the Wakde-Sarmi campaign. The port of Sarmi, about 150 miles northwest of Hollandia on the New Guinea coast was taken in a land invasion while the Wakde Island, only a few miles offshore, was taken by a Marine landing, both actions beginning May 23rd. Unknown to me at the time, the part of our combat team that had been at Wakde was sent on to Biak in the Schouten Islands, about 200 miles northwest of Sarmi. During the invasion there, a Japanese suicide squad over-ran the 147th's position, causing considerable material damage, wounding some of the men, and killing Bill Ross, my Ballarat 'adoptee brother' and frequent tent mate. That fateful day was May 30, 1944. Colonel Scurr, commanding the 147th, was observing the battle at the time and helped in directing artillery fire from a cave.

By June 3rd, the 158 RCT, complete with all of the 147th, had been ordered to move back from the Sarmi-Wakde-Biak area to conduct longer-range artillery fire on identified targets and provide harassing nighttime shelling to discourage Japanese snipers and night attacks. I was not sure of our position, other than in the jungle, but presumably it was near the northernmost point of Dutch New Guinea, with exception of the Vogelkop peninsula. Besides getting the guns into position, we developed a perimeter defense, strung barbed wire, laid mines, set booby traps, etc. By June 5th we were ready for the attacks that all expected and on that day a Japanese bombing raid destroyed our two observation-liaison planes (L-4). Losing those planes made artillery firing very difficult since observation and fire direction had to come from forward observers on the ground in the jungle.

CHAPTER TWELVE
Jumping Off

On June 30th the 158th RCT, commanded by Scurr, departed New Guinea for the last time, headed for Noemfoor Island in the Japen Strait. This island is almost midway between heavily fortified Japanese stronghold at Manokwari on the Vogelkop peninsula and the formerly held Japanese base at Biak. That meant we were making a stab deep into Japanese held territory, and moving directly toward the Philippine Islands. As we cruised, our convoy grew and the consensus of opinion among us was: "Finally we are getting the support that Roosevelt promised while we were yet in Darwin more than two years before."

As we approached the northwest shore in early morning darkness on July 2, U.S. Army planes bombed the Japanese air base near our landing spot, with the Navy's rocket-firing converted destroyers joining in. I do not know how many Army bombers were involved, they were very low and close together, nor do I know how many Navy ships were equipped with rocket launchers, but the bombardment was so intense that the deck of the ship I stood on shook and quivered, and the explosions ashore were so close together that it was almost a deafening roar. The assorted ships and landing craft moved ashore almost enmasse, under cover of darkness and smoke. To make this the most ideal invasion I was ever involved with, the LSI (landing ship infantry) went right up onto the beach so that we did not have to wade ashore. Being with an artillery observation party, I would accompany the infantry in a landing, so as to be where the infantry was, when and if artillery fire was needed. Obviously the

An Unexpected Journey

guns would come ashore later. Just as in the previous island-hopping excursions, a primary objective here was the air base. The U.S. bombers were operating from bases and landing fields in Australia, whereas the fighter planes, with much shorter travel ability, could join the bombers when they reached islands much nearer the Japanese targets; then after the raid was completed, the fighter planes could drop out again at the island airstrips (that we had taken and were protecting) from which they came. In the case of Noemfoor, aerial photographs revealed a well-developed Japanese airport along a beach on the north side of the island. Because this island, like most of the East Indies islands, was covered with thick jungle and had a rugged interior, it had been decided to circle around and attack from the north where the packed coral airstrips and improved beaches were. When the assault battalion, to which I was assigned, came ashore there appeared to be no Japanese resistance and we set up a 158th Infantry command center alongside the airport runway. Infantry squads immediately combed the surrounding area and found few living Japanese but many dead. It surprised me that anything could have survived the bombardment and shelling. There were many caves dug into the coral alongside and near the airstrip, in some were bodies of the enemy, apparently killed by concussion. Damaged and abandoned equipment was everywhere. Work began almost as soon as we landed, clearing away wreckage, dredging out the coral by the shore to allow more landing craft a closer approach and filling bomb craters in the airstrip. The mopping up by our infantry was nearing completion when the LVT (Landing Vehicle Tank) brought our howitzers ashore about noon. I was observing the process until I heard on the command post radio a message that: "General MacArthur had ordered the 503rd Airborne Infantry to reinforce a faltering beachhead at Noemfoor". With due respect to the well-planned and executed invasion thus far, I was stunned and insulted to hear "faltering beachhead". I was there, no living enemy was there, and all work was progressing far better than anyone should have expected. Never having witnessed an airborne infantry landing, I ran out to the landing strip to watch.

The planes came so very low that I could see the paratroopers' faces as they jumped. When their chutes opened, most of the men were jerked violently and were so near the ground that they could not get into a good position for landing or to get control of their parachute. Several were in such a position (ie., upside down) that when the chute opened the abrupt jerk caused their helmet strap to break. If that didn't break a person's neck (and maybe it did sometimes), it would sure hurt. One of those falling helmets came directly my way and I barely jumped aside before it crashed into the coral runway. I don't know how many planeloads or how many paratroopers were involved. I did see some men falling on top of others who were unable to rise or were too slow to get up. Several fell onto the shattered stumps of trees near the landing strip, and at least one landed astraddle of one of the oak bows of a truck which had the canvas cover removed. This was a most painful thing to see. I helped get him off and to the medic aid station.

To my mind, this entire paratroop operation was the most uncalled for, the worst conducted, and greatest abuse of personnel that I ever saw. Practically all of the paratroopers had painful landings, some fatal. The majority landed out of control on the packed coral runway, either bouncing once or twice or bouncing and sliding,

An Ulvog Journey

dragged by their parachute. I helped several to their medical center which was set up by the first to land and, after the drop was over, asked one of the medics how many of the group survived 'battle ready'. His estimate was about 50. Since their camp was set up next to ours and bustled with activity that evening, I sauntered over to see how they were faring. Those were the 'well physically fit' of the group and most were limping or had bandages on various body parts. None of them were out on patrol or perimeter defense. It sure changed any ideas I might have entertained about the glamour or glory of paratrooping.

In the meantime our infantry (158th) had pretty well cleared a large area near the airport, encountering only scattered Japanese rifle fire, and had not needed artillery support. July 4th we moved to an area somewhat farther inland and, I believe, toward the east where a rise in elevation and a clearing in the jungle made for better gun positions. Here we set up a close perimeter defense using machine guns and mortars as well as rifles. The howitzers had also registered (adjusted) fire on several suspected Japanese sites, so all in all it was a good RCT set up. Although it did seem as though this required a great amount of work, which we would likely soon move away from, it turned out to be a very good investment. In early morning darkness July 5th the first and most ferocious Japanese attack since our landing here, came as a surprise. The infantry called for artillery and mortar fire almost immediately and, because of the previous day's preparation, that was provided. The first waves of the attackers were almost totally cut down, but a few suicide warriors attempted to cross our perimeter shortly afterwards. Machine gun and rifle fire stopped these. It was all over for the day when the fog and mist cleared away in the morning. There may have been a few badly wounded Japanese taken prisoners, I only saw many dead.

After this short but violent morning wake-up call, everything calmed down. Small infantry squads, usually accompanied by an artillery observer, patrolled farther ahead of the main camp every day. I often went along on some of these patrols since I am not by nature a 'spectator-sport' type; ie., I'd rather be a player than a watcher. By now I had come to know and appreciate many of the 158th Infantrymen. Some of them, possibly most, had seen combat duty previously either in the regular army or in mobilized reserve call-up. They had earned their own insignia (snake coiled on a bolo knife) and the regimental name "Bushmasters", due to distinguished service in Panama jungles, home of the largest poisonous snake known, the Bushmaster. Many clearly showed traces of Aztec or Inca lineage so it was no surprise to learn they preferred close-quarter combat, especially with knives or bayonets. In general, they did not take to rest camps well and, after a day or two of boredom, invented sports or games such as: One man would take his bayonet from its sheath in the tent, run out in the company street and challenge any and all to try to take it from him. Invariably, his compadres would come rushing out, literally competing for the chance to take the knife from the 'mad' man waving it and having hands and arms cut in the process. I did not mind accompanying these folks on a patrol because they took pains to protect their source of "the big stuff" should they need it. I was always placed near the rear of the column, near machine gunners and mortar men during a march.

An Unexpected Journey

CHAPTER THIRTEEN
Getting The Picture

On one memorable patrol we came to a small stream, probably a mile or more from camp. Scouts and squad leaders agreed that some Japanese had recently been there and I radioed this information to our command post. Proceeding for a short time along a faint path up hill in the direction that the scouts indicated the Japs had gone, we suddenly received the signal to 'take cover'. The scouts at the head of the column were out of sight to those like myself at the rear, but we tried to hide near the trail not knowing exactly why. After what seemed to be hours of silence there were some scuffling sounds ahead followed by the 'all clear' and 'assembly' signals. Three Japanese soldiers with rifles on their shoulders and with numerous empty canteens (bottles) strung on the rifle barrels, had been seen or heard coming down the path, obviously to get water. Those Bushmasters were very much in their element and had no doubt employed this tactic before. The four or five men leading our column remained silent and hidden as the enemy passed by. Then from behind one of our group silently clamped his hand over the mouth of the rear most Japanese and simultaneously cut his throat. In rapid succession two other Bushmasters performed identical procedures on the two remaining Japanese. Not a word was said, hardly a sound made. The three almost decapitated bodies were quietly dropped on the trail, I sent the radio message to camp and we all hastily returned there, all the while expecting some enemy retaliation. I was really thankful that I was on the team with the Arizona boys, not against them.

The 503rd Airborne was engaged in clearing out the enemy on the south half of the island while the 158 RCT was mopping up the north half, where we began the invasion. The paratroopers did not have artillery, of course, and I got the feeling they were not impressed with the heavy guns. It seemed to me they were a young, cocky lot that had exaggerated opinions of their abilities. Nevertheless, the 147th was assigned to them for artillery support, which meant we had to have gun positions that allowed firing on the entire island, fifteen miles long and twelve miles wide. Because of the dense jungle and hilly interior our three batteries were placed in three widely separated positions. As a result communication was a real problem and at times it was necessary to relay messages and fire control data from one battery to another through the L4 (Liaison plane). On one occasion the plane's observer spotted a building with nearby activity. Although this potential enemy target was located in either A or B Battery's zone for defense, their forward observation parties were patrolling at that time. So it was decided that a detachment of the 158th Combat Team would investigate and I, as a C Battery instrument man, would join in the patrol. Other than hacking our way through some jungle growth and wading in some streams, we eventually, with help from the L4, came in sight of a large building of mostly jungle material, standing coconut trees for corners and side bracing, bamboo floors, braided palm leaves on the roof, etc. The palm leaf walls were about four feet high, the rest open, and the floor about 18 inches above ground level. We cautiously encircled this place at some distance and then closed in. The stench was nauseating.

An Ulvog Journey

Sounds of moaning and muffled painful calls came from within, but no sign of an upright person. I was on the back side of the building when shouting began in front, followed by several rifle shots, then the signal to jump into the building, guns at the ready. I did not get into the place because when I looked over the half-wall the scene sort of paralyzed me. There was just one open space or room. Lying about in various positions were many emaciated humans, all terribly sick and some obviously dead. There was just one Japanese soldier guarding the front entrance, shot dead by one of the Bushmasters. It was apparent to us that he had been left there to guard against anyone coming to or leaving from that 'hospital'. Papers found in his uniform confirmed that. We helped get out all of those abandoned slave laborers and cleaned them up as best we could while awaiting help from our medics. Practically all had been lying in vomit and excrement and were covered with flies. None could stand or walk unaided. We discovered that they either had a broken foot or leg or had been bayoneted through the foot or both. I did not count either the living or dead, nor could I sleep for many nights afterwards. Eventually we learned that the Japanese Army had taken about 1000 prisoners from Formosa and more than 3000 from Java to Noemfoor as slave laborers. Less than half of the Formosans were found alive by advancing American forces and only 400 of the Javanese, all with wounds, sickness and showing starvation. I do not know the nationalities of those we liberated or how many survived, but my impression was that there were more dead in that jungle prison than came out alive. Due to the many reports from all of the East Indies islands concerning evidence of extreme cruelty by Japanese conquerors, neither American nor Australian soldiers were inclined to risk taking prisoners. All of those in the infantry and anyone apt to contact the enemy in person had a card in their helmet with words or letters, the sounds of which supposedly translated the surrender call into Japanese. It seldom worked.

In the book <u>South Dakota in World War II</u>, Colonel Scurr writes: "Over half of 550 Formosans who voluntarily surrendered were hospitalized for malnutrition and tropical diseases. Those who were captured (by the Japanese) said their original number was 400 and at least one third (300) died because of overwork, inadequate food and untreated disease. The Javanese suffered even more horribly than the Formosans. According to surviving Javanese captives, 3,000 men, women and children were rounded up on Java and shipped to Noemfoor where they were forced to work on roads and airdromes by hand. They were denied adequate food and shelter and refused medical care. When caught starving and stealing food they were beheaded or hanged by hands or feet until they died. Of the 3,000 brought from Java only 403 survived." According to Robert R. Smith in <u>Approach to the Philippines</u>, "the physical conditions of these survivors defied description."

During active operations on Noemfoor Island, patrolling infantrymen discovered Japanese bodies with portions of flesh cut away. After an increasingly large number of these evidences of cannibalism were found, bodies of American dead were also discovered, again with much flesh having been cut away.

Another patrol turned out to be less nauseating and far more enjoyable. By this time, mid-July, most of the organized enemy resistance had been wiped out. Nevertheless patrolling squads tended to be "trigger happy" and very cautious.

An Unexpected Journey

We had not gone far from our bivouac area until we came to a fairly good trail that headed pretty much in the direction we had planned to go. All went well until the scouts spotted a building or structure ahead. The silent signal went down our column, "disperse, surround target, and take cover". While the usual tropical island style of construction had been used (palm leaf roofing and partial walls, coconut tree corners and upright wall bracing, etc.) this building was higher than usual. Surprise; no one was there, inside or outside.

Instead it was a supply depot, stacked to the roof on one side and the back with cases of saki (rice wine or liquor). The cases, well made of wood, held probably fifteen quart-sized bottles each. The glass bottles had been beautifully wrapped in straw and packed with more loose straw in the boxes. I would guess there were several hundred cases, maybe a thousand, stacked here. Taking turns guarding against a surprise Japanese return and helping ourselves to as many bottles of wine as we could carry, we planted several mortar shells and some primacord (fuse-like explosive) amongst the crates in the building. Then after retiring to a safe place the fuse was activated. The fireworks display was dazzling, so much so that we were forced into a further hasty retreat. Too bad no one had a camera along. When we returned to the bivouac area there was quite a party. The next morning many headaches taught the lesson that this 'fire water' was designed to drive the Japanese soldiers fighting mad, literally.

By August 31, 1944, Noemfoor was declared free of Japanese troops, although later reports said a few individuals had been found living in isolated parts of the interior. The 147th now was reunited and developed a tent camp, complete with coral floors and walkways, and even enclosed showers and laundry rooms. Rotation to the U.S. of 147th personnel had been going on ever since we were in Darwin, but now this was speeded up. As new replacements arrived they were soon integrated into the 'old style' artillery training, even though we had not been in any combat situation where genuine field artillery practice could be used.

So, in spite of the dense jungle, forward observation parties were sent out and, because occasional Japanese sightings were reported, small infantry patrols accompanied us. As luck would have it, a group that I was with did encounter a few of these enemy survivors. We were walking along a well-beaten path, not being particularly quiet when the advance scouts gave the "take cover" signal. Alongside the trail on the downhill side was a hollowed out pocket in the dirt, much like the 'blowouts' in the sand hill country. Roots from trees along the sides protruded into the cavity, except on the opening facing the trail. I had not seen anything unusual here before getting behind a tree. Most of our column had almost passed this 45' to 50' wide cavity before a scout saw or heard movement. After we were deployed, probably in a few seconds, one of the infantrymen shouted out the standard call, in Japanese, "drop your weapons, come out with hands above your heads, and you will be treated according to terms of the Geneva Convention". The thirteen enemy soldiers who had been hiding, all jumped up and began scrambling and crawling up the walls, pulling themselves up by the root sticking out. They all had rifles but kept them slung over their shoulders. It was very obvious they had no intention of surrendering so everyone in our group fired until no movement in that hollow could be

An Ulvog Journey

seen. Our squad leader, a combat tested Bushmaster, ordered his men to strip search the bullet riddled enemy while we observers reported to fire direction center by radio and received the, "Mission completed, return to headquarters" response. This was my last forward observation tour on Noemfoor. I cannot erase from my memory the sight of those Japanese warriors scrambling to escape like so many rats caught in a box. Why didn't they open fire on us? Why didn't they surrender? Maybe they were drunk on saki?

CHAPTER FOURTEEN
Leaving the Indies

On December 29, 1944 the 158th RCT left Noemfoor, headed for the Philippine Islands as part of General MacArthur's 6th Army. The 158th was split into three or four groups, divided somewhat along battery organizations, that is, each battery with its contingent of infantry on separate ships. Presumably it was for the purpose of speedier landing and fast deployment. It seemed to be another case of compounded confusion. As we apparently wandered aimlessly around in the open sea, more 6th Army ships joined the ragged convoy. Everything fell into place, however, when we approached Luzon, the main island of the Philippines. The ship carrying Battery C of the 147th and its contingent of the 158th Infantry was the first to land in Lingayen Gulf on the northwest side of Luzon. So here I was on January 11, 1945, along with the first group of Americans to set foot on the island where Manila is located, where the Battan Death March began in 1941. Actually our landing was designated as D+ 2, meaning 2 days before MacArthur. One of the first ashore was Colonel Scurr who picked out the locations for all of the 147th gun emplacements and that evening our guns began firing on Japanese targets. It was a busy day. The next morning we started our advance to the north, pretty much following the coast along the Damortis-Rosario Road. I was with the 158th Infantry in a FOP (forward observer party) during most of the East Indies and Philippines campaign so was rarely with our firing batteries when they moved. Unlike the terrains we had become accustomed to in the three years of foreign duty to date (swamps, jungle, etc.) we were now in fairly open dry country where, as Colonel Scurr put it, "We can again do field artillery by the book." Progress was relatively slow due to intermittent shelling by Japanese guns. It seemed as if this was intended to deter possible beach landings, as most of the shells landed there. The infantry would run into Japanese fortifications at some of the town sites and the 147th howitzers then wiped them out, along with most of the town, which the Philippines had evacuated. At several places, enemy guns targeted the road itself and as we reached those particular points, a hail of large artillery shells would greet us. As a sort of comedy act, most of these large projectiles were duds and, upon hitting the paved road, either bounced, slid, or gouged out a deep trench. Inspection revealed that the detonators (fuses) were missing and, in some cases, the loading ring was still in the nose. The gun crews were, in effect, shooting cannon balls.

As we advanced toward Rosario, known as the Philippine Summer Capitol, the terrain was increasingly hilly with steep ridges and wooded valleys, sometimes with patches of cleared farmland. The Japanese had obviously expected an attacker

An Unexpected Journey

to come up the coast highway, just as we were doing, because they had dug in artillery pieces, machine gun posts, mortar mounts, and grenade launchers on the back (north) sides of the hilltop ridges with small grass covered openings on the front facing us. Some of the larger gun emplacements were caves deep enough for the gun to be pushed up to the opening for firing and then pulled back into the cave, canvas or burlap covering the large cave opening. One or more of these housed railway guns, complete with rails long enough for moving the gun itself in and out of the cave-tunnel. There were also some naval guns hidden in such caves. Several times when we were pinned down by such installations it was necessary to coordinate all of the 147th howitzers with naval guns offshore and Army Air Force bombers to literally rake an entire mountain ridge. In one such instance, we had been at the crest of one hill for a night and about half of the next day. As soon as one or more infantrymen attempted to go over the top, heavy rifle fire cut them down. While attempting to locate the enemy positions with the L-4 planes and coordinating all of the 147th guns for massive concentrated fire we were all just in or near our trenches dug the night before. I had long since learned to dig a six-foot long trench about eight inches deep and carefully pack all of the rock and dirt excavated along one edge and end. Then I'd have another FO member dig his trench alongside and line his edge and end likewise. Since I packed the radio I preferred that my trench partner carry the battery power pack. Hooking them together, the radio became my pillow for night service. Even with very low volume, vibrations of an incoming message awakened me. Observations of bomb craters and point-detonating artillery excavations, told me that dirt and rock on top of the ground was almost as effective as solid ground in stopping fragments of exploding shells. Hence my "lazy man's foxhole". On this particular day, the battery-pack carrier was new to forward observer operations and had been assigned here because he appeared to be extremely tense and nervous around the howitzers, especially during firing. He seemed eager to learn and I tried to calm him. We were sitting on the edge of our trench making small talk while awaiting radio messages when suddenly a grenade flew over the ridge, landed ten or fifteen feet directly in front of us and rolled on down the hill. My partner literally froze; staring 'bug-eyed' at the obvious dud, and without a word fell over. A couple of Bushmaster medics came and put him on a stretcher. As they started downhill he was crying, screaming, bleeding from nose and ears, urinating, kicking and waving. The medics had apparently seen it all before; "psycho" they said. I never saw the boy again. Later in discussing this with our doctors they explained, "His nerves were so stressed that while awaiting the explosion, which didn't come, they just snapped."

    Eventually we were able to get over this ridge and after crossing a fairly heavily wooded valley there was another ridge and another shelling from the north. We again dug in for the night. This one was different. The previous night firing by the Japanese had been rather erratic, inaccurate and light.

    On this night they must have had us pretty well located because regular shelling by mortars, grenades and artillery hit in the general area of our forward position. As far as I know, there were no fatalities among the 147th or the 158th people, although flying steel fragments caused some injuries. What really made this a night to remember was the landing of a large artillery projectile some fifteen or twenty feet

An Ulvog Journey

from my trench. It was, obviously, a dud probably fired from one of the American coastal guns captured at Corregidor. It was about one foot in diameter and two feet or more in length. When it hit the dirt, it was at an angle which caused it to plow a furrow about eight feet long in a curved path so that it went underground and came part way back out. Dirt and rocks flew pretty far when that thing hit, some onto me. It might have been getting hit by the dirt that woke me but I really think it was the shock wave through the ground. I was so wide-awake that I made note of the date, January 17th.

The three firing batteries were quite widely separated and were apparently all on different missions or different schedules, although all headed in a generally northerly direction toward Rosario. It was very confusing because of the erratic artillery bursts that seemed to surround us, some, of course, were from the Japanese guns. At times small enemy groups would manage to slip past forward 158 RCT perimeter defenses and cause a number of causalities, some fatalities, before being stopped. According to our medic's records, the combat team had 300 men wounded severely enough to be out of action, plus 50 killed in the first week of our advance. All firing batteries' forward observation parties were involved. The day after the heavy shelling and the near direct hit by the big dud, a combined bombardment and shelling of the valley and mountain ridge ahead of us by Naval guns, Air Force bombs and our artillery left little probability of enemy resistance. Much of the artillery shelling involved phosphorus projectiles, which caused most of the grass and shrubbery in the valley and on the hillside to be burned away. There must have been tons of explosives and steel fragments poured onto that ridge. When we crossed the area, rapidly upon the halt in shelling and with a fair amount of smoldering vegetation providing us cover, it was frequently as if we were in a plowed field. It was here that we saw the total Japanese determination that no one would pass. Beyond the valley, along the slopes of the hill facing our position were many holes. In each was a Japanese soldier with a rifle, a box of food on which he could sit and a can of water, (maybe a bottle of Saki too?) The dirt from excavating these holes was nowhere in evidence, and the grass had been allowed, or encouraged to grow right up to the hole's edge. With the rifleman seated in the hole and with a canvas-covered helmet, his detection from the air or ground was impossible. When standing and resting his rifle on the ground amongst the grasses he was a deadly sniper. I paused momentarily at one of these 'burned off holes and relieved the corpse of his rifle. Later I learned that there were actually two ridges, named the Red and Blue, somewhat offset from each other but both leading to the same mountain mass. I don't know which ridge I was on. However, the next day it was decided that we would have to clear the enemy out of their strongholds on and beyond those ridges. In retrospect, I have concluded that this was undoubtedly the nearest I came to the "bullet with my name on it". We had gone down into a mountain valley where a stream was running. We walked uphill in this quiet little brook for a ways. I'll never forget that peaceful place, for a group of Philippine women and children coming down from the mountain were paused in the shade by the stream where they reached out and took by the hand (everyone who permitted it) and kissed it before passing the hand along to the next woman in line to do likewise. No words that I understood were heard; any necessary?

An Unexpected Journey

Shortly after this little meeting we started up the slope of the mountain, which was relatively free of brush, no trees, but good grass cover. As usual, I was with the FO party, carrying the radio, and was about two-thirds of the way to the ridge top when (pardon the French) all hell broke loose. The Japs had apparently been alerted and were ready for us. Our Bushmaster called for "cover" (which seemed superfluous) and the entire hillside was soon covered with running Americans, bursting mortar shells and exploding grenades, I just slid the radio and backpack around to the front, wrapped my arms around it and rolled downhill, hoping the power-pack carrier would follow. Actually he passed by me when I headed toward a large uprooted tree stump for readjusting my load. When I got behind this 'bullet stopper' I found one of my Bushmaster buddies there. He had been shot through both cheeks and the tongue with tooth parts sprinkled around in the blood. Obviously he could not talk. I called for medics, then helped lay him down and talked to him, telling him I would give him water to wash out his mouth (what was left of it) but not to swallow it. After I used all the water in my canteen, he indicated I should go and he would lie still until the medics came. Then I rolled on down the hill, I don't know his name, I could only hope that the medics reached him in time, I also hope that he was not being carried on a stretcher a short time later when they passed us down at the brook hooking up the radio, because an explosion downstream was thought to be approximately at the location where the medics might be. In the morning another combat team of the Sixth Army joined forces with the 158th and, with assistance from Navy guns and Army air bombers, managed to take control of some of the mountaintops. There was so much action and shifting of positions that I pretty much lost track of time. It seemed as if we were involved in firing missions day and night, everything was confusing, but we were now up on a mountain and not facing another broad valley as before.

It was generally known that Lingayen Gulf was to be MacArthur's entry point on Luzon and that our job was to make sure that the Japanese forces (known to be entrenched in the mountains to the north) could not come down to stop that entry or cut off the supplies to support the landing. The main body of MacArthur's force was to drive south to Manila, of course. As we proceeded northward, the generals in command named prominent surface features, and such names were adopted for all military maps in the area. One general, reported to be MacNider, had been reading a new book named "Forever Amber" and declared it to be the dirtiest, nastiest book ever. He named the depression between the Blue and Red ridges "The Forever Amber Pass" because he said that was where occurred the dirtiest, meanest fighting he had seen.

The mountainous terrain was fairly well timbered and grass covered, with small relatively shallow depressions and low hills. Apparently we were getting close to Rosario. We had heard from some of the Philippine guerillas we contacted that the government moved there from Manila to escape the heat and humidity for a month or more during the summer, and Rosario was in very pleasant mountain surroundings. I never saw it, nor do I think the Bushmasters actually got there. We had too much fighting to do. On one night's shelling by the enemy I stopped a piece of mortar or artillery shell, which did not fully awaken me. It was obviously spent and merely

An Ulvog Journey

falling, cutting my poncho and trouser leg and making a light slash in my thigh. In the morning I saw the tear in the clothing but didn't know what had happened until I rose up and saw the piece of iron fall out. The cut had bled enough to form a clot so I just got a medic to cover it. In a couple of days it was OK.

The plan for FOP personnel was by the book, five days with the infantry at the 'front' and ten days back at the battery where new clothes and equipment would be provided if and as needed. Also bathing and self-serve laundry was part of the R&R (rest and recreation). In actual practice, however, the 'cycle' usually got switched, so more often it was ten days on FO and five days off. We were always short of people, so most worked in some way while not in combat.

While the climate and semi-forested terrain was a welcome change, the attitude of the enemy went from mean to savage. On one forward probing patrol we came upon a vineyard, complete with a long, narrow building with a tin trough about 18 inches wide, two to three feet high along one wall and fronted by a wooden shelf, much like a kitchen counter by a sink. This was on a gently sloping hillside with a flue of bamboo bringing water from a stream into the tin trough. It was obvious from some clothing and utensils scattered about that we had surprised a few very recent inhabitants. There were 20 or 30 trigger-happy GI's looking for them, without finding any. About forty feet downhill from the grape-processing shed was a grassy little ditch or ravine. The scouts searched this cautiously without raising anyone, but did find, by probing the tall grass along the banks, some openings, obviously caves. After a conference above the ditch and radio messages to headquarters, it was decided to set fire to the grass in the ditch. Going into the caves could be suicide, of course.

There was a large tree up on the knoll where we were somewhat assembled and shortly after the grass was set on fire, we saw smoke up in the tree. Ah ha, a vent from a cave below. Now the cave opening along the ditch bank was easily seen, and before long coughing could be heard. Ever faithful to the Geneva Accords, a Bushmaster stood by the cave opening and made the surrender call. His answer was a grenade flying out. He was quick enough to escape being injured but there were many rifles at the ready just above the cave opening. Another surrender call, this time from above, got the same reply. A scout on the opposite bank fired a smoke grenade from his rifle launcher into the cave, whereupon we heard much coughing, grenade explosions, rifle shots and shouting. Then, with bayonets fixed, one Japanese after another came running out screaming and each in turn were riddled with Bushmaster firing. Twenty-three of them all in a pile and I don't know how many dead were inside. By now more caves had been spotted so after radioing Headquarters we made a hasty retreat. In the morning, after laying down an artillery barrage on the winery location, we returned with a larger group and with "track-layers", bulldozer tractors equipped with flame throwers. We were met with rifle fire and grenades at first, but with our mortar fire and rifle grenades, we were soon in control of the area. The clean up then consisted of one Bushmaster crawling up alongside a cave opening and calling out for surrender. If a grenade or rifle shots came back or if there was no response, the flamethrower sent a burst into the cave and then promptly plugged it with dirt using the bulldozer blade.

This was the last action I saw while on FO duty with the 158th RCT. The

An Unexpected Journey

147th was pulled back almost to Damortis where we could still provide artillery support to the Rosario area if needed, but also help protect Lingayen Gulf from possible Japanese attacks while the main invasion forces landed. It was a continuation of our "holding if not eliminating" the heavily armed Japanese troops known to be dug in to the north.

On February 13th, 1945 the 158th RCT was relieved of its one-month's tour of essentially day and night combat duty and sent to a R&R (rest and recreation) camp near Tarlac, about sixty miles southeast of the Damortis station and, like Manila, located on the main highway to Luzon. This camp was set up on what had been an airport that had been captured by the American and Australian troops now fighting in and around Manila. Located on the large Central Plain of the island, it was a most welcome change from so much of the jungle, forests and swamps we had endured in Australia, New Guinea and other Indies islands. I don't remember much about this camp spot except that I finally cured the fungus that had affected my feet. I never knew the correct medical name, but this rash-like disease was called "jungle rot" by all of us in the Southwest Pacific. It was somewhat like "athlete's foot" because it usually started on the feet but, if not treated and stopped, would spread. I had seen hospital cases where the "jungle rot" had practically destroyed the skin on a person's feet and part way up their legs; obviously a crippling, painful condition. So now that we were in an open, sunny, dry locality I took a cue from the natives—go barefoot. However, I did not go unshod away from our developed camp because I had seen too many cases of elephantiasis among natives on islands of the East Indies.

CHAPTER FIFTEEN
Job Change

Two weeks or so after coming to the Tarlac rest camp (frankly, I don't remember the 'recreation' part), the 158th RCT was ordered to take control of the Batangas Bay area about 125 miles to the south and some 60 miles south of Manila. This meant we would have to pass through Manila, where the main invasion forces of MacArthur's Sixth Army had reportedly captured the capitol and were 'mopping up' the surrounding area. As our convoy was rushing through the city, I was riding in an open jeep. There were still the sounds of sporadic rifle fire and explosions of grenades and/or mortars but no apparent attacks on the convoy. However, little flying metal particles hit me in the head. Just my luck, spend a month out in the country where iron and lead chunks flew day and night without scratching me, and get shot just passing through town! One little piece got into my eye, and another in my eyebrow and some more elsewhere in my head (all of them are still there.) So my early days at Batangas were spent in a hastily thrown up field hospital, with my eye swelled shut. The doctor said X-rays showed where the fragments were and, after the swelling went down, he could get them out. However, when I could open my eye, he said it would be wise not to disturb it for a while. He said the scar was dormant, showing no signs of growth, which would be common in such injuries. He also said if such growth did occur, possibly from a surgery to remove the splinter, it would likely continue until a cataract formed. In that case 'shaving' the eyeball would be needed periodically to

An Ulvog Journey

maintain my sight. So we left it alone. (Lady luck smiled again; the scar has remained dormant.) For a while that eye did not focus or see clearly, resulting in my inability to use the FO binocular field glasses. The battery supply officer, a good friend who had been in fire direction school with me and had the same rating as I, suggested we trade jobs. Our company commander agreed that this would be an excellent move. So from then on, in early March, I was the supply officer.

It turned out that the Batangas Bay area was heavily fortified by the Japanese and the RCT was hard pressed to clear the area, mainly because of entrenched Japanese artillery in a mountain and lake complex inland to the northeast. So once more an airborne infantry was flown in to help the 158th. This time I did not see the 'drop' close up, but did see some of the bruised and battered infantrymen brought to the hospital. That reinforced my conviction that walking, although slower, was really less painful than falling from the sky. There were numerous movements of the 147th gun positions because of terrain problems but our base (HQ) camp stayed in one position, as I recall.

There were always attempts by Japanese to infiltrate any and all gun emplacements or other posts by night, usually by individuals or teams of two. Every group position, therefore, had to develop a perimeter defense, the manning of which was a burden. No longer being with a FOP, I usually spent the nights in a perimeter defense spot, where two or more persons took turns watching for infiltrators. One night I shared a machine gun 'nest' with a best friend who had grown wise to the ways of the 'night crawling' Japs. In the middle of the night, while I was sound asleep, he began kicking me. Of course, talk was simply outlawed in such situations. When I crept up to him he whispered and pointed. "Look at that water buffalo", he said, "See anything wrong?" No, I didn't, it was just walking slowly and maybe aimlessly. He whispered, "Look closely." Then he pressed the trigger. There was a big, bright, loud explosion about 150 feet in front of us, where the water buffalo had been. The infiltrators had learned how to bend low next to these "beasts of burden", prod and steer them to where they wanted to go, walking with them and keeping in step with their leg movements. They invariably had on vests of high explosives, set off with a built-in trigger. The target could be a gun emplacement, a truck, a personnel encampment, a supply dump or other large object where they would get close and blow up themselves in the process of destroying their target. It was, and had been for a long time, the unwritten but understood law amongst us all: "After dark no American or Australian moves. If nature chances to call, your trench or foxhole becomes your latrine." A hard lesson but it can save your life.

At the ending of March 1945, the Bay of Batangas and adjoining sea coasts had been cleared of Japanese troops and guns and the 158th RCT was once more on the move. This date I remember because it was on April 1 [April Fools Day]. We landed at the port of Legaspi in Albay Gulf, 175 air-miles east-southeast of Batangas, and well over 200 miles by road. This is at the far southeast end of Luzon on the Sorsogon Peninsula and near the famous Mayon Volcano. Being in charge of Battery C Supply section, I no longer went on FO duty or Bushmaster patrols. Sadly, my friend who was so eager to take my place on the FOP, was killed just three days after we arrived at Legaspi. In his one month or less at FO duty he had received a field

An Unexpected Journey

commission (lieutenant), which I had rejected. I am haunted by the thought, "What if I had escaped the flying iron in Manila?"

One of the tasks, not ordinarily delegated to the supply department, was the matter of laundry and clothing repair. In rest camp and in non-combatant bivouacs this chore was generally individual responsibility, but now, because of the demands of artillery fire missions and perimeter defense, it became company (battery) concern. There were many women and children in Japanese-occupied lands who were left destitute when the men either fled to join guerilla groups in the mountains or were taken prisoners, and these people were eager to do any sort of work to earn an income. A man who had been a professor at the University of Manila (now in ruins) had become a sort of entrepreneur and sought out employment for them. Philippine customs forbade or discouraged women to approach or speak to strangers, so this man acted on their behalf. He came to our camp almost before we were settled and was brought to me where we worked out a tentative agreement on the matter of laundry, subject to approval by my company commander and by his group of laborers. It worked out well. He would pick up the soiled clothing at my tent and distribute it to the women at the camp entrance. When the laundry was finished, the man would return it. This became a weekly routine. I do not recall the pay scale, but I do recall that the clothing had not only been well cleaned and pressed but if it had been torn or a button missing upon pickup, it was repaired and the button replaced when it came back. I don't know where or how the pressing was done, where the buttons came from or where patching was obtained. However, I know where the washing took place; at a river or stream nearby. I eventually went out to the women and children one day to compliment them on the great job they were doing. Apparently this made a big hit with them because, through their ex-professor boss, my superior officers and I were invited to a certain house in town for a dinner prepared by our washerwomen.

When the company commander got the message, I was alternately praised (for diplomacy) and damned (for the invitation). We had long since been told we must be civil and polite toward our hosts and allies and, in almost the same breath, to never ever eat native-grown food. Sanitation as Americans understood it, simply did not exist. So, since declining an invitation would be an insult, it was determined that the two of us, the captain and I, would go and hopefully we would be able to get back to camp before we became violently ill.

The house, apparently the home of one of the laundering group, was less than a mile from camp and did not seem to have been damaged by shelling. Like most dwellings, it was on stilts or posts with a space beneath the floor of eight to ten feet in height. Neatly stacked here were piles of dung and vegetation waste. When rice-planting time came, this material would be spread on the paddy and mixed into the soupy mud. We had already learned, from observation, that natives here do not wear shoes or sandals in their houses so, after climbing the stairs we removed our shoes and socks, putting them alongside the other footwear on the porch before entering. I do not know if all of the washer group was there, but could have been, there were many and only three men. The ex-professor/organizer escorted the two Battery C guests. I'm sure the women had on some of their finest clothes and they all bustled about getting the table ready. Then the three of us men were ushered from the parlor to the dining room where our hands and feet were washed and dried before the serving began. I do not know what most of the food was, with the exception of the rice, but it was delicious. There must have been three or four of the women 'waitering' on each of us, urging us to more of everything. After we finished, again came finger washing, then back to the parlor for some small talk. All in all, it was a great dinner with gracious hosts. Big surprise, we did not get sick! I would have to rate this event a highlight of my stay in the Philippines.

A 'spin-off of all of this was that I became very well acquainted with the professor and he would invite me to accompany him as he visited various friends in town. On one such visit we called on a very refined lady who had obviously lived an above-average income style, but whose husband had been taken captive when the Japanese invaded some three or more years before. Presumably he was dead, and she had gone into sewing, dressmaking and such to earn a living. After the first few visits, along with my professor-entrepreneur friend, I was invited to her house alone, first for a dinner and later on presumed business calls. In telling of some experiences I'd had in the Indies islands and the Philippines, this lady asked if I had ever seen any Japanese parachutes. Of course I had and, in fact, I had one in my duffle bag at the time; I had tried to use it as a bed sheet, one time. She said that she would like to have some of it, and I assured her she could have it all. To show her appreciation she wanted to make me a Philippine 'party shirt' from some of it. This led to requests, through our mutual professor friend, for me to come to her house for shirt measurements. After having tried on the body section of the shirt it became apparent to me that this gal might just have something more in mind than a shirt.

One day I got the message that my shirt was almost finished and only needed some more measuring. As luck would have it, the 147th was alerted to prepare for a move. I advised the 'professor-turned-promoter' we would be terminating the laundry contract and to advise the lady dressmaker friend that I would try to see her shortly. I never went back.

On May 25, 1945 the 147th moved to rest camp in the vicinity of Legaspi but quite removed from our former 'battle station'. I never got to the Mayon Volcano or to any of the towns where we had been before, including Legaspi, except to Manila itself. At that point there were very few, probably 10 or less of the original 147th group that left the U.S. in November 1941, still with it. They were all, including me, transferred to a camp at Manila to await transportation to the United States. The 158th RCT was now attached to the Eighth Army preparing for the invasion of Japan. For a few days, my stay at the Manila depot was plain boredom, but eventually I was put in charge of a warehouse where Philippine workers (mostly women) were engaged in cutting up American military boots and reducing clothing to cleaning rags. Much of this appeared to be new and unused. It was the most depressing time of my military service to be involved in such a waste.

In mid-June the long awaited trip towards home began. I am not sure of the date, I don't remember the name of the ship and can only recall the name of one other shipmate, another original 147th man. After a long cruise and many stops we arrived at Newport News, Virginia. There the shipload of returning servicemen was divided into different groups, probably based on their destinations. The group I was

An Unexpected Journey

with went by railway on July 24th to Leavenworth, Kansas, where we had health inspections, were given some earned medals and some individuals were discharged. One other 147th rotated man and I did not receive orders for discharge; there may have been others. When we complained, we were told that the Leavenworth station did not handle discharges; only sent those entitled to such to the proper discharge center, which in our case would have been Fort Snelling. However they said that the records for our service were incomplete so we were assigned to a replacement center at Camp Bowie, Texas. After complaining to other officers, we got the same response, but we were given a one month Delay Enroute to report there.

Upon reaching home I learned that my father had passed away and my older brother had been seriously wounded in the Allied invasion of Germany. That was a jolt, far from the homecoming I had expected. My friend and I did report to the Texas camp as ordered, getting there about the end of August. We were assigned as drill sergeants to train new recruits. Marching and similar parade ground drills were by now almost as foreign to us as to the rookies. It didn't apply in what we had done in the past 3 1/2 years. Many of my days were spent harassing personnel officers concerning their failure to honor the far more numerous points (credits) that I had earned that warranted discharge. Being at a replacement center had all the potential of my being sent back overseas. Possibly because I was a 'thorn in the side' of the personnel department at Bowie, I was shipped to Fort Sill, Oklahoma, where I was promptly assigned to teach artillery fire direction. However, I was determined to get what was rightly mine, so I continued demanding my discharge here also. At the time Fort Sill was not qualified as a discharge center, but did become one about a week later. Three others and I were the first ones to be discharged there in October. So, after almost five years, my intended "one-year adventure" came to an end.

An Ulvog Journey

147th Field Artillery – 158th RCT

<u>Action Sequence</u>

Fort Ord	12/17/40
Furlough – US	
Angel Island	11/16/41
Honolulu	11/27/41
Equator	
Darwin	1/6/42
Alice Springs	7/3/42
Ballarat	7/8/42
Melbourne	8/1/42
Brisbane	10/9/42
Rockhampton	2/23/43 – 3/5/43
New Guinea	7/27/43
Sydney	Hospital
Ballarat	Hospital
Canberra	Hospital
New Guinea	Hospital
Kiriwina	11/26/43
Finchhaven	4/5/44
Sidney	Hospital
Ballarat	Hospital
Hollandia	
Biak Island	
Sarmi	
Nooemfoer	7/2/44
Japen Island	
Lingayan (Luzon)	1/11/45
Damortis – Rosario Road	
Tarlac	2/14/45
Manilla	
Batanges	3/2/45
Lemery	3/8/45
Tarlac	3/12/45
Lemery	3/14/45
San Miguel (Hospital)	3/25/45
Batangas (Supply)	4/4/45
Legaspi	4/8/45
Manilla	4/30/45
Ft Sill, OK	
Discharged	9/18/45

An Unexpected Journey

Editor note: A photocopy of the following award is in the book An Unexpected Adventure:

By direction of the President

THE BRONZE STAR MEDAL

Is presented to

STAFF SERGEANT CARL G. ULVOG

United States Army

For heroic achievement in connection with military operations against the enemy in the vicinity of Damorits, Luzon, Philippine Islands on 17 January 1945. Sergeant Ulvog, a member of an artillery Forward Observation Party, was serving with an Infantry Assault Company which was ambushed by the enemy while attempting to advance up the steep slopes of the Red Ridge. Although the company was forced to withdraw hastily, he remained at the artillery radio position assisting in its operation. Then dismantling the radio and with the aid of another member of the Party, carried the power pack unit of the radio to the rear in the face of intense enemy small arms and mortar fire, thus saving a very valuable piece of equipment which was highly instrumental in directing accurate artillery fire on the enemy during the ensuing attack. Sergeant Ulvog's personal courage and keen devotion to duty reflect great credit to himself and the military service.

An Ulvog Journey

Reading About Your Own Funeral

James Ulvog

Your editor moved to Albuquerque, New Mexico way back in 1982. When I visited Uncle Carl and Aunt Dorothy at their home in Santa Fe, New Mexico, he always told many stories. Uncle Carl was a wonderful story teller, which having just finished reading of his unexpected adventure around the South Pacific you can now appreciate.

On one of the earliest visits, he told of his experiences during the war. One of them was barely mentioned in the story you just finished. I'd like to share it with you in more detail.

The ship carrying Uncle Carl and his battalion left Pearl Harbor on December 1st or 2nd, 1941. At the time of the Japanese attack on Hawaii, the convoy was on its way to Guam, which was also hit.

The convey consisted of unarmed merchant ships, with no Navy escorts. Thus, there were no big guns to protect the troopships. Since the 147th Field Artillery and their gear was on board, the commanders realized they did actually have some guns available. As you read, the troops pulled their artillery pieces out of the hold, lashed them to the deck, and practiced firing at drums in the water.

How effective that would have been against a submarine or surface ship is debatable, but at least the convey had something, however little, for defense. The troops also had lots of work to do so they could keep busy for a while.

Well, that still leaves a convoy of ships and a bunch of soldiers floating around somewhere in the Pacific with no particular place to go. Recall Carl observing the shadow of the ship's mast go in circles on the deck of the ship because the ship was going in circles.

To protect the convey and all the men on board, the Navy announced that all those ships had been at Pearl Harbor and were 'presumed lost', which means lost with all hands on board.

Telegrams were sent to all the families, with the standard condolences on the loss of your loved one.

Yes, that means that grandma, grandpa, and all the siblings were told their beloved son and brother was lost in battle. The family held a memorial service and worked through their grief.

That seems a rather cruel lie, telling the families of 500 or so members of the guard unit and all the other families of all the other troops on all the ships that their loved one had died. Since this was a South Dakota National Guard unit, all those troops would have been from the state. Image the concentrated loss throughout the state.

Think of it a different way.

That grief was a small price to pay in order for there to be plenty of public knowledge that the ships were on the bottom of the harbor instead of floating

An Unexpected Journey

somewhere at sea. As a result, the Japanese did not learn there was an undefended convoy out there somewhere, ripe for sinking at leisure. So, they didn't know to look for such a juicy target and didn't bother trying to find ships they would have thought were on the bottom of the harbor.

When mail service was established in Darwin, Australia, the unit learned they had been proclaimed lost. This was mentioned briefly in chapter 5. Carl was able to read the newspaper announcement for his own funeral, something very few people get to do.

An Ulvog Journey

Postscript to *An Unexpected Adventure*

Editor note: At Christmastime, 2000, I sent a letter to Uncle Carl thanking him for his book. I encouraged him to write an expanded version to share with his family. He replied with the following letter, which I cherish because it such a beautiful illustration of the modesty and self-restraint of Daniel and Lydia's children.

Uncle Gilbert returned with serious physical injuries, which you have read about. Uncle Carl returned with back injuries you haven't read of.

This letter also reminds me of the tremendous sacrifice paid by those who came back apparently whole. Some who returned were crippled emotionally. To all those injured in the mind we also owe a debt of gratitude.

Uncle Carl's letter:

Jan 20, 2001

Dear Jim:

Thanks for the letter and the salute. Must say that is (was) a surprise; very unusual in this age of pretty much ignoring (at best) or reprehending (at worst) a person's wartime service for his country....

Apparently you realized that the blood and gore was pretty much filtered out of my 1940-1945 report. An expanded version, which others besides yourself have requested, would contain a good bit of that nightmare stuff; not really pleasant reading. It took me most of my spare time in 1988 to write and rewrite what eventually became the book which went to my children and siblings. I have been able to attend almost all of the reunions that my artillery unit has held for the past 45 years; one every five years on average. While I didn't think I could manage the trip this past fall (it's always been in SD) three cousins arranged to get me there and back. So I went and glad of it; this was the last one. Too many of the bunch have answered their last roll call.

Too often in the past, at work, church, or other gatherings, I've casually mentioned going to these reunions, and it was usually met with a remark such as: "why waste your time and money just to gad around with a bunch of drunken old ex soldiers." So I just don't talk about it. If you haven't been through the "meat grinder," you can't understand.

Thanks again for thoughtful message. Sorry if I got to 'preaching' again.
Yes, I've been blessed by God many times over. It's like a cartoon someone sent me: "God isn't finished with you yet."
Best regards & love, Carl

Mom's Memories

Section 3

MOM'S MEMORIES
Louise Sherrick

Editor note: This story was written by Aunt Louise. She sent the editor a copy in November 2008. Date it was written is not readily known. The original manuscript was typed in all upper case. It has been scanned and converted to upper and lower case. The text has been edited only slightly to retain Louise's conversational voice.

Lloyd wanted a black doll, and my mom got one for him. We had a wooden cradle that the babies slept in. I believe it was made by Grandpa Ven. Don't know what happened to it.

We had an organ we pumped with our feet. I never took any music lessons, but I'd go and sit and play songs from memory. It filled my heart with joy. About the only songs I knew were from church.

One year for Christmas, mom made green (mint) dresses with white collars and cuffs. We sang a duet in church (St. Paul's). Christmas was special for us when we'd go to Sunday school program and get a sack of candy and an apple or orange. Sometimes we would go to 2 churches and receive the same from them. We didn't have a Christmas tree or gifts. Our Christmas meant celebrating the birth of Jesus.

When I was in 7th or 8th grade, Lucille Disbrow gave me the tree we had at school and I dragged it two miles home. We had nothing to put on it nor under it, but we had a tree.

When we were in younger grades, living north and east of Elk Point, dad would take us to Coyote school with the team of horses and either the lumber wagon or sleigh. Dad had a big black fur coat. We had a horse-hide hair robe to cover us up with.

One of my greatest joys was going to Grandma Ven's house. Prior to Grandpa Jim Ven's death, we'd go there and dad would have us sing. We'd stand in the door of grandpa's room. I was probably 6 or 7 years old when he died (*Editor note: probably about 1928 or 1929*). The last part of his life, a bed was put in the front room for him. All of mom's family was there, sleeping on the floor (all over). Each of mom's family would kneel by his bed to say good bye. He said he could hear the angels singing. At the cemetery, Ardis Womblom fell near the grave. Her mom had made her aware of germs, and ordered her to be careful. She'd wash door knobs, etc. She would give Alice and me some of her clothes. We were pretty happy to get them.

Grandma Ven would take me with her to gather eggs (chicken house, granary, barn, and out in the grove). In the spring, hens would lay eggs in little metal chicken houses. When they hatched, grandma put a fence in front of the door so the hens wouldn't get out and wander about. But the chicks would get out.

Grandma taught me the joy of picking up sticks. When grandma came to

An Ulvog Journey

our house to stay, she'd sleep between Alice and me, in our bed. Early on she taught us the Lord's Prayer in Norwegian.

Mom's wedding dress was decorated with beads, which she had sewed on. On mom & dad's 25th wedding anniversary, I had my picture taken wearing her wedding dress...I wonder where it is? When I find it, I will take it to the Elk Point museum.

Mom & dad never had a vacation.

When she was expecting a new baby, we didn't know about it. I remember mom laying Clarice on a pillow. I never knew how much she weighed. We would go visit, both Alice & I would want to hold that baby. I think Clarice Mae was named after Aunt Clara, but not sure.

Clarice was 7, when I got married. I really did not know her that well. She did stay with us, on south Henry Street, so that she could finish high school. That was when she met Bob Patterson. He was a bell hop downtown.

Dad sang in the St. Paul choir. On the nights he went for choir practice, we would help mom with the milking chores.

That brings up the cream separator and how we had to wash that out. If we added too much soap to the water, it got stringing and icky! It was a big job in itself, to wash all those cyliners.etc... (and they say woman's work is a snap? No way!)

Back then, women didn't work outside the home. House work was a full time job.

Our Aunt Hanna was a nurse. When we came home from school one day, she met us at the door, with:" hush! There is a new baby in the house! We were all born at home. I remember when Jim was born, tongue-tied. Mom & dad took him to the doctor to take care of that. He was probably the only one of us who ever went to the dr. He sure looked cute in his new baby clothes!

Mom used to get clothes from Aunt Rose & Aunt Hanna. She would make them over for Alice & me. Mom made most of our clothes until we learned to sew. Sometimes we would have dresses made with the same pattern, but different print fabric. All sorts of things were made with the sacks that chicken feed came in, like aprons and towels, etc.

I remember mom had a box of powder in her drawer. Grandpa had sold Raleigh products. Boy, that powder sure smelled good! We never had perfume.

We ate around a round wooden table. The youngest sat next to dad. I never liked oatmeal. So when there were three younger than me, I quit eating oatmeal.

When mom was expecting (Clarice), Gilbert always said it would be a boy. But Alice and I wanted a sister. Gilbert was the one to announce that we got a baby sister! She was so small!

Back then, eggs were 10 cents a dozen. A loaf of bread was 5 cents. Gasoline was 10 cents a gallon (for those who had cars). I remember 2 cars that were out in the grove at grandma's - Ole Gunderson & Chris Gunderson's old cars. (Grandma Randi's brothers). We would sit in those cars and take pretend trips often.

We had Fords, usually. On Saturday nights, we were lucky; we could ride along with dad, when he and mom went for groceries. He would bring eggs & cream to the creamery. Aunt Elsie worked at the grocery store, before she married Joe. It

Mom's Memories

was common practice to hand the clerk your order, and come back later, when it was filled. In those days, it was safe to walk the streets. (Can't say that these days.)

For the most part, we knew just about everybody. Divorces were pretty much unheard of (also rape or incest, or child abuse or homicide, or alcohol or drugs). Families were a close knit unit, as God intended them to be. When grandma came to stay, it was great joy in our home!

We didn't have any luxuries, as we didn't know what they were. We had food, shelter and love, with a Christian environment. Prayer and family worship are needed for a good life. I feel our home had these qualities.

We moved many times, generally in March, by wagon or hayrack (for the furniture). We would get to our new home, and have to set up beds, so we could sleep fit the first night. It was hectic, but dad was a good planner. Our 1st move was after we lost our farm during the depression. I think I was in 2nd or 3rd Grade (*Editor note: that would put loss of the farm in about 1930 or 1931*). We moved to the Talley farm, on the highway, going north, out of Elk Point. We left Coyote school for Peterson school. (Now the school was moved, and that corner is a gravel pit. On the corner we turned left, to go to St. Paul church.) I felt like we were moving to a new country! Little Did I realize that I would still have the same friends at Sunday School and church.

At that time, Rev. Amouth was our minister.

I believe we moved to Hurley, South Dakota after that. That was a long move. I do not know how dad found these farms. We were bused to school here. We went to Scandia church. Clarice was born at this time. We had wood burning stoves. That meant somebody had to chop wood, and keep the wood box filled.

We had no radios during the 20's. Our social life was visiting our relatives. Mom always brought along something to go with coffee. Quite often we went to Grandma & Grandpa Ven's, or to Uncle Knute & Clara's.

We all had chores to do. Mine was cleaning and filling the kerosene lamps (no electricity). One day, it was getting late, and mom asked why I'd waited so long to fill the lamps...my reply was "in case tomorrow doesn't come, I have not done it in vain!" (Smart mouth!)

Mom's work was the usual baking bread, washing, ironing (the old flat iron, which I still have) and cleaning, which was usually done on Saturday. I remember Alice & I would argue over who would do the upstairs or down stairs. On one day, I was cleaning upstairs with a broom. I had all the dust swept to the top of the stairs. When Alice opened the stair well door to ask how I was doing, I swept the dirt down the stairs!!

Sunday was always a day of worship. The Lord truly blessed us and our country, for which we are thankful. When we sat in church, we were to sit quietly, not wiggling our feet or whispering. My dad was strict, for which I am thankful. Most important was that he was a total Christian.

Farm work was very time-consuming. Horses were used for everything. Tractors, corn pickers, & hay loaders were just beginning to make an advent upon the farm scene. Before winter, the ground had to be prepared. In fall, there was corn to be picked. That is were Alice met Mervin (when she & I were out, picking corn).

An Ulvog Journey

Dad had hired 2 neighbors to help. Mervin was one of them about 1942.

Our stay on the farm with all the hard work, tempered us for latter life. It was an education in itself. At the onset of the "great depression", we were geared to accept even less. Today, we sometimes drive our car unnecessarily. Sometimes we go up town for just one thing. If dad was going to town, he would always ask mom what she needed from the store.

I remember if mom knew she wouldn't have time to make the bread, she would have dad bring home some. I can remember seeing mom with one arm holding a baby to nurse, while the other arm was kneading the bread! We loved the bread and rolls mom made. But when we had store-bought bread, we'd sit at the table and just feel it. It was so much softer! On rare occasions, when we had rolls from the store, one by one (of us kids) would take out a roll and lick the frosting off the cellophane sack, and put it back on. Mom would say: "it works, every time!" She knew each of us would do the same thing.

When we were eating supper, dad would tell Alice and me to be sure to do the dishes. Well, we'd say "there isn't any hot water, so we'll do them in the morning." then dad would say that we were pretty smart, since we knew mom would have them done in the morning! Dad got smart, and made sure there was hot water on the stove when we sat down to eat!!

There was a section on the end of the stove, called the reservoir, I think, and the stove would heat that water. Of course we had to add water to it. We brought in water from the cistern, to use for washing dishes, shampooing and bathing.

We had a big galvanized wash tub for bathing. Just imagine having to lift that tub of water to throw it out! It was probably mom who got that chore. She really deserved a gold medal, for raising 8 children!

Perhaps the greatest blessing of all was the ability to travel without horses, to our friends and relatives. There, we mixed with Christian fellowship, the ingredient necessary in our lives…often lacking in today's busy lifestyle. Today, TV occupies so much of our time. Club meetings and organizational meetings, etc. take up so much time. We don't take the time to visit friends or family anymore. Our many "time-saving" devices give us more free time, but where does that time go???

People, who lived during my growing up era, were plain, ordinary, good people. Most seemed to possess certain values and concerns for the family. I know I am thankful to God for a loving Christian Family.

When we lived on the home place, one of Annabelle's boys bought it. We lived across the field from the county farm, where Hoflings lived. So I knew that family well. They came to Centerville on a cold, snowy day, for my 18th birthday. Pop told Isadore to drive, because of the ice. Mum (Dagmar) Dorothy & Isadore came. Mom had fixed a lovely dinner and it was love at first sight for Isadore & me. We began corresponding and dating, and were married the following year, on Feb. 2 (ground hog day). Isadore's friend, Garold Ellyson, and Alice were our only attendants. We were married in Nebraska.

No honeymoon for us. We had secured an apartment in Sioux City, 1609 Pierce St. It had a Murphy bed which pulled out of the wall. Isadore worked at J. C. Penney in the men's dept. Penney's gave us a blanket, and we bought our tableware

Mom's Memories

(2 forks, 2 knives, & 2 spoons). Mom had (used) dishes for us. We bought pillows and sheets. It was a very humble beginning, but I was not used to having very much.

Love was blind and wonderful. I was sooo happy! I'm certain I got pregnant on our wedding night. We stayed at Hoflings. So I was pregnant during the hot summer. Isadore was called to the service, and I delivered a breach baby girl, who died during my convulsions. We named her Alice Louise. She was buried in the Hofling lot at St. Paul church.

Isadore got a leave, to come home. I was in bed so long, I had to learn to walk all over again. My feet flew up in the air! It was a sad time. I had made flannel baby clothes, including diapers. How many girls do that today?

Later, I got a job in Sioux City. I wanted an office job, but got hired at Cudaheys, with 59 cents an hour, stamping bologna & "Thuringer" (a hard Salami-like ring, with darker meat). The language was so bad to hear, that I left and took a waitress job at the Arcadia. Mr. Schaffer, the owner, died the morning Isadore came home from the service.

We took a train trip to Denver, Colorado. I wore lots of hats, and took 7 hats with me on this trip. Boy! Was I "green"! We got caught up, looking for a home and a job, which there were none.

Section 4

Economic Life on a Farm in the 1940s
James Ulvog

The probate documents filed to settle the estate of Daniel Ulvog provide an opportunity to peer into life on a South Dakota farm in 1945 and 1946. It also provides many insights to how hard life was at the time.

The discussion which follows was published on the editor's blog in 2019 and 2020. The posts have been modified slightly for this book.

Picture of life on a South Dakota farm based on what can be seen in a probate document

In 1945 my paternal grandfather departed this vail of tears. The probate document filed for his estate the next year provides a financial glimpse of life on a South Dakota farm in the mid-1940s.

This was a time of low productivity with all the members of a large family working all day every day to keep the farm running.

Farmers were starting to transition from horse power to tractor power.

It was also a time of self-sufficiency: Raising the oats and hay to feed the horses to work the fields to raise the corn and hay to feed the pigs and cows to sell for money to pay for the farm.

I will use my accountant eyes to see what can be learned from just a probate filing.

Glimpse into economic life on a farm in 1945 provided by probate documents

My paternal grandfather passed away on June 1, 1945, near the end of World War 2.

Disposition of his estate was officially approved by a court, which provides us a glimpse into the economics of farm life in the 1940s.

He died intestate, meaning he did not have a will, so the estate was distributed in accordance with South Dakota state law. His estate went through probate, which means a court had to approve the distribution.

The filing with the court contains a list of:
- income
- expenses,
- unpaid bills,
- inventory of estate assets, and

An Ulvog Journey

- distribution plan of the estate assets.

Including in the filing are a number of references to the prices of animals and a few references to price of personal property. Looks like most of my grandparent's minimal wealth was in the farm stock.

As a result, the court filing allows us to study the economics of one farm in South Dakota from June 1, 1945, which is the day my grandfather died, through April 2, 1946 when the accounting was filed with the court. That 10 month period of time covers one harvest and one round of birthing animals, which is essentially a farm year.

From all of that information, I can piece together a balance sheet for the day my grandfather died and the day the estate was probated. I can also make a guess at an income statement for the intervening months.

A series of blog posts will explore what we can learn from studying the filing.

Prices of farm animals in 1945

The probate filing for the estate of my grandfather, Daniel Ulvog, provides a lot of information about the farm. Let's look at indicators of the price of farm animals. The filling provides a number of data points.

Here is the listed information sorted by animal with a mean (weighted average), mode (price with largest number of animals), and my point estimate of the price of different animals.

Cows:

Sales:
- $132.07 - 19 head

Purchases:
- $50.00 - "1 cow"; oddly low price suggests this was not a mature cow
- $43.74 - "one cow"; again, this does not appear to be mature cow

Appraised value:
- $30.00 - 25 calves,

A calf is under 1 year of age. A yearling is between 1 and 2 years old. (The distinction is something this city boy had to look up – please don't laugh at me!)

The $30 price is mentioned as calves. The $50.00 and $43.74 proceed appear to be yearlings. This leaves $132.07 as the sole indicator of mature cow prices, which is a good indicator since there were 19 head sold at the time.

Estimate of prices

So, I will use these prices:
- $132 - cow
- $47 - yearling (average of two data points)
- $30 - calf

Mixture of ages:

Purchase:
- $167.50 - one cow and one calf

Economic Life on a Farm

This price now makes sense and supports the above prices. One cow at $132 plus a calf at $30 would be $162, which is close to the purchase price of $167.50.

Hogs:

Sales:
- $35.31 - 3 hogs
- $57.78 - 11 hogs
- $50.00 - sale of hogs without indication of number sold - assumed to be 2 based on prices

Inventory:
- $45.50 - 13 hogs at appraised value

Estimates of prices

Calculated prices:
- $49.41 - mean (weighted average)
- $45.50 - mode (data point with largest number of animals)
- $51.12 - mean of two largest data points

The $35.31 price seems to be an outlier, possibly because those 3 animals were smaller or younger. Thus I will use mean of two larger items, which is:
- $51 - hog

Recap

I will use these prices for animals:
- $132 - cow
- $47 - yearling
- $30 - calf
- $51 - hog

Cash transactions listed in 1945 probate filing

The estate of my paternal grandfather went through probate in 1946 after he died in 1945. The probate filing listed the cash received and paid from the time of his death until the document was filed with the court.

The filing provides a view of farm life in the mid-1940s. This series of posts uses the filing to take a glimpse into life back then.

Here are the cash transactions listed in the court filing:

Cash received

Date	Description	Amount
6/1/1945	balance of cash at death	391.26
6/29/1945	sold 19 head of cattle	2,309.32
10/5/1945	sold 3 hogs	105.94
10/29/1945	sold 11 hogs	635.62
12/24/1945	sell hogs (number not listed)	100.00
1/22/1946	Cooperative Oil Co. gas dividend	60.14
2/23/1946	Sell International Truck	600.00

An Ulvog Journey

3/13/1946	Income from plowing	110.00
3/23/1946	Loan repayment	90.00
	total cash received	4,602.28

Cash disbursed

9/1/1945	Yankton Production Credit loan payment	(2,103.76)
9/17/1945	Cemetery lot	(15.00)
9/22/1945	household furniture	(79.95)
9/27/1945	surety bond	(40.00)
10/2/1945	insurance assessment	(3.00)
10/2/1945	Cooperative Oil, gas and oil	(28.07)
10/9/1945	Montgomery Ward, clothing	(2.46)
10/9/1945	Sears, tires for trailer	(55.42)
10/10/1945	Cooperative Oil, gas and oil	(21.17)
10/12/1945	Montgomery Ward, clothing, repairs	(12.87)
11/13/1945	Cooperative Oil, gas and oil	(47.12)
11/15/1945	Cooperative Oil, gas and oil	(49.65)
11/27/1945	Cooperative Oil, gas and oil	(20.26)
12/11/1945	Wass Funeral Home, funeral	(366.23)
12/26/1945	Cooperative Oil, gas and oil	(17.50)
1/14/1946	Cooperative Oil, gas and oil	(16.10)
1/15/1946	chickens purchased	(162.50)
1/22/1946	purchase 1 cow	(50.00)
1/23/1946	groceries	(9.60)
1/26/1946	veterinary fees	(7.50)
2/6/1946	purchase 1 cow	(43.75)
2/8/1946	coal	(14.00)
2/9/1946	coal	(23.70)
2/11/1946	Cooperative Oil, gas and oil	(16.00)
2/12/1946	one cow and one calf	(167.50)
2/13/1946	Loan to one of the children	(90.00)
2/15/1946	purchase hammer mill	(91.00)
2/22/1946	shelling and hauling corn	(113.13)
2/25/1946	linoleum	(46.12)

Economic Life on a Farm

2/26/1946	Cooperative Oil, gas and oil	(18.70)
3/4/1946	last half of 1945 taxes	(31.74)
3/4/1946	cash rent for 80 acres, 1946	500.00)
3/4/1946	clerk of court, filing fees	(17.50)
3/9/1946	life insurance assessment	(3.00)
3/16/1946	Vermillion Plain Talk, publication	(17.36)
3/27/1946	Attorney fees	(299.90)
3/27/1946	exchange on checks	(0.72)
1945-1946	total cash disbursed	(4,602.28)

Cash-based income statement of farm in 1945/1946

Above section lists the cash transactions in the estate of my paternal grandfather from the day he passed away until a probate filing was prepared for the court.

As you read the summarized income statement and cash transactions below, keep in mind this is the cash activity to feed and clothe a family consisting of one mom and four children still living at home. Notice was one purchase of groceries for $9.60 and only two purchases of clothing. There is no indication of any purchases in November or December which could be considered Christmas presents.

To say finances were tight would be an understatement.

The cash transactions can be summarized into a cash-based income statement as follows:

Cash, June 1, 1945	391.26
proceeds from selling assets	3,950.88
income	110.00
purchase of assets, primarily animals	(514.75)
farming expenses	(176.05)
taxes paid	(31.74)
land rent, 80 acres	(500.00)
housing expense	(157.72)
gas and oil purchased	(174.43)
coal purchased	(37.70)
loan payment	(2,103.76)
final expenses (attny, funeral)	(755.99)
Cash, March 27, 1946	-0-

First estimate of value of my grandfather's estate at close of probate

An Ulvog Journey

The probate document for my paternal grandfather listed the assets in his estate. What is the total value of his estate? Let's ponder that question.

Values for some items are listed in the probate document. Prices of asset purchases and sales during the time between his death and filing of probate document can be used to estimate other values. For example, I estimated values for livestock above.

Here is a summary of the assets:

livestock	4,508
oats and corn	1,794
tractors	450
tractor drawn equipment	150
horses	400
horse drawn equipment	140
other equipment	180
car	300
total assets, without $400 liability	7,922

My estimate for the value of the individual items in his estate as listed in the probate filing are accumulated below.

item	quantity	price	value	
cows	15	132	$1,980	A
bull	1	100	100	B
yearling	14	47	658	A
calves	25	30	750	B
spring pigs	20	51	1,020	A
horses	4	100	400	C
John Deere Model D tractor	1	300	300	B
John Deere Model B tractor	1	150	150	D
John Deere cultivator	1	50	50	C
three bottom (plow?)	1	50	50	C
2 bottom plow	1	50	50	C
"other old machinery"	-	-	??	
binder (horse drawn)	1	20	20	C
disk mower (horse drawn)	2	20	40	C
plows (horse drawn)	2	20	40	C
stacker (horse drawn)	1	20	20	C

Economic Life on a Farm

hayrake (horse drawn)	1	20	20	C
small tools	1	10	10	C
elevator & hoist	1	30	30	C
manure spreader	1	20	20	C
wagons	2	50	100	C
hay rake	1	20	20	C
1936 Ford V-8 Sedan	1	300	300	G
(car had heater *and* radio!)				
new hay, stacks,	2	?	???	E
hay, tons	7	?	???	E
household furniture				
corn, bushels	800	1.24	992	F
oats, bushels	1000	0.802	802	F
assets			7,922	
liabilities				
administratrix fees (to Lydia)			(400)	B
net worth			$7,522	

Notes for source of value:
A – Calculated based on transactions described in probate document
B – Value listed in probate document
C – Wild guess
D – Guess based on the Model D being the largest in the Deere product lineup
E – No idea on how to estimate value
F – "Fred" database from St Louis Fed
G – Guess in relation to $600 sales price of truck

    An unknown number of chickens at an unknown price per head is not included above. Probably should include $163 on the basis that the many dozens of chicks are worth at least as much as was paid for them three months earlier. Probate filing does not give a count of the number of chicks or full grown chickens.
    My goal is to eventually roll this book to the date of his death. There is a long list of assumptions I have to work through to back into those valuations.

    The St. Louis Federal Reserve Bank maintains a database with an astounding range of information, to include crop prices and production levels by years, going back decades and decades. That is the source of the market prices for corn and oats.
Corn prices obtained from the "Fred" database:

An Ulvog Journey

- June 1945 - $1.18/bushel - Wholesale Price of Corn for Chicago, Il. - https://fred.stlouisfed.org/series/M04005US16980M280NNBR
- April 1946 - $1.24/bushel - Wholesale Price of Corn for Chicago, Il. - https://fred.stlouisfed.org/series/M04005US16980M280NNBR

Oat prices:
- June 1945 - $0.711/bushel - Wholesale Price of Oats for Chicago, Il. - https://fred.stlouisfed.org/series/M04074US16980M261NNBR
- April 1946 - $0.802/bushel - Wholesale Price of Oats for Chicago, Il. - https://fred.stlouisfed.org/series/M04074US16980M261NNBR

The values above are somewhat soft, especially the various pieces of farm equipment. Here is a breakout of how the numbers were developed, which shows most of the valuation is firm, with only about $1,300 consisting of estimates or guesses:

Basis of valuations:

Mention in filing or calculated based on specific numbers	4,808	64%
Market prices for St Louis Fed	1,794	24%
Estimate in relation to other prices in probate filing	450	6%
Wild guesses	870	12%
Specific liability mentioned	(400)	-5%
Estimated value of estate at close of probate	7,522	100%

Economic life on a farm in 1945: family size

My grandmother, Lydia (nee Ven) Ulvog was 52 years old when the probate document for my grandfather's estate was filed.

At the time of filing the probate document, the children of Lydia and Daniel were:

- Gilbert, age 29, recuperating at DeWitt General Hospital in Auburn, California as a result of injuries received the winter of 1944 during the Battle of the Bulge in Germany.
- Carl, age 27, stationed in Bowie, Texas awaiting discharge from the army after fighting in the South Pacific. If President Truman had not authorized use of nuclear weapons against Japan, Uncle Carl would have instead participated in the invasion of Japan with a good chance of either having been killed or severely wounded.
- Alice, age 25, married and living with her sister in Sioux City since her husband was fighting overseas.
- Louise, age 21, married and living with Alice, since her husband was also overseas.
- Lloyd, age 19, still living on the farm.
- Olaf, age 17, still on the farm.

Economic Life on a Farm

- James, age 13.
- Clarice, age 9.

Yes, that is eight children with a 20 year span of ages. That is also a glimpse of life on the farm in the 1940s and probably for hundreds of years before.

The two oldest 'boys' were off in the army, not to return home until later in '46 or '47. The two oldest 'girls' were married with both their husbands also off at war. Three boys, ages 19 through 13 were at home along with their youngest sister.

That means after grandpa Daniel died grandma Lydia ran the farm with only three teenage boys and a preteen girl.

That would have been quite a challenge because before the war, in '41, grandpa and grandma ran the farm with the help of children aged 25, 22, 20, 16, 14, 12, 8, and 4.

That means the available hands to help with the work on the farm shrank:
- 1941 - 5 adults (over 19) and 4 teens or younger (excluding a 4 year old)
- 1946 - 3 adults and 4 teens or younger.

That is a severe drop in labor back when farming was drastically more labor intensive than today.

I'm a bit fuzzy whether my grandparents farmed 360 acres or 80 acres. Regardless, they ran the farm with the help of eight children.

One of my cousins lives on a farm. Her husband and son run over a thousand acres by themselves in their spare time. That is an astounding improvement in productivity over the last 70 years.

Consumer price index from 1940 through 2019

For an indicator of the changes in prices from the World War 2 era through today I pulled CPI information from the Bureau of Labor Statistics.

This info will roll into my comments on the probate document for my grandfather's estate. It is also useful for general information.

The furthest into the table I can link is here: https://data.bls.gov/cgi-bin/surveymost?

The data is the CPI for All Urban Consumers (CPI-U) from 1940 through 2019 from Series Id: CUUR0000SA0.

Select data:

Year	Jan	Jul	Oct
1940	13.9	14.0	14.0
1941	14.1	14.7	15.3
1945	17.8	18.1	18.1
1946	18.2	19.8	20.8
1950	23.5	24.1	24.6

1960	29.3	29.6	29.8
1970	37.8	39.0	39.4
1980	77.8	82.7	84.8
1990	127.4	130.4	133.5
2000	168.8	172.8	174.0
2010	216.7	218.0	218.7
2019	251.7	256.6	257.3

For future reference, that shows inflation on a nationwide basis for urban consumers calculated as follows:

CPI index July 1946	19.8
CPI index October 2019	257.3
ratio	12.997
rounded	13.000

The inflation was 1200% in that time frame, which means a basket of stuff costing $1.00 in July 1946 would have cost $13.00 in October 2019.

Adjustment of prices from 1946 to 2019

Is there some way to adjust the prices described in my grandfather's 1946 probate document into today's dollars?

Developing some way to compare prices across time is always a challenge. A few prices to describe the challenge:
- $146 - value of a cow in 1946
- $300 - value of a 1936 Ford V-8 sedan, nice enough to mention it had a heater AND radio
- $300 - John Deere Model D tractor, the then largest tractor in the Deere line
- $56.70 - monthly pay rate for corporal (E-2) with over 3 years service
- $69.30 - monthly pay rate for sergeant (E-3) with over 5 years service

How do we convert those prices into something we can appreciate today?

A post not included in this book describes the pay of soldiers during WWII to now, with a calculation of the ratio between the two. Previous discussion lists the Consumer Price Index - All Urban Consumers from the 1940s through today.

Neither of the comparisons are perfect. First, the relative pay for members of the armed services was increased dramatically during the 1980s and 1990s. During that time I was on active duty many of the enlisted troops qualified for food stamps. An increase by factor of around 33 for the enlisted troops and around 26 for officers is an overstatement. That means the proportionate increase for soldiers is not a great reference point.

The consumer price index has increased by a factor of 13 fold between July

Economic Life on a Farm

1946 and October 2019. That is not an ideal price indicator because the concept behind it is an average urban consumer. Prices for farmers, particularly when in near subsistence, would not necessarily correspond. However that is probably one of the better indicators we have.

Bringing those two factors together shows the relative relationship of those two indicators as follows:
- 33x - approximate increase for enlisted soldiers
- 13x - consumer price index increase for urban consumers
- 2.75x - ratio of higher increase for enlisted troops than general urban consumers, which actually is in the range of plausible based on my gut feel

So, I will look at the inventory of my grandfather's estate using multiplayer increase of 13 fold. In other words $1 in July 1946 will be adjusted to $13 today.

Guess at value of 1946 estate expressed in 2019 dollars

The values assigned to my grandfather's estate when it was probated are listed earlier.

My determination of a adjustment factor of 13 to bring 1946 prices forward to today is shown above.

The extended string of assumptions I've made shows a rough guess of the estate:
- 1946- worth $8,085 gross, with $7,785 after the administratrix fee due to my grandmother.
- 2019 - worth about $105,000 gross and about $100,000 after the only listed liability.

Detail of the assets are:

	1946 $ each	1946 $ total	2019 $ each	2019 $ total
cows	132	1,980	1,716	25,740
bull	100	100	1,300	1,300
yearling	47	658	611	8,554
calves	30	750	390	9,750
spring pigs	51	1,020	663	13,260
chickens		163		2,119
horses		400		5,200
John Deere Model D tractor		300		3,900
John Deere Model B tractor		150		1,950
John Deere cultivator		50		650

An Ulvog Journey

three bottom (plow?)		50		650
2 bottom plow		50		650
"other old machinery"		?		-
binder (horse drawn)		20		260
disk mower (horse drawn)		40		520
plows (horse drawn)		40		520
stacker (horse drawn)		20		260
hayrake (horse drawn)		20		260
small tools		10		130
elevator & hoist		30		390
manure spreader		20		260
wagons		100		1,300
hay rake		20		260
1936 Ford V-8 Sedan		300		3,900
new hay, stacks,		???		???
hay, tons		???		???
household furniture		???		???
corn, bushels	1.24	992	16	12,896
oats, bushels	0.80	802	10	10,426
assets		8,085		105,105
administratrix fees (to Lydia)		(400)		(5,200)
estimated net worth		7,685		99,905

More thoughts about life on a farm in 1946

Been thinking more on what life was like on the farm after my grandfather passed away.

Consider the cash expenses again - notice there are no bills for electricity, telephone, water, or sewer. Such things weren't in place. My grandparents, aunts, and uncles lived without electricity or running water or sewer systems.

I'll guess seed and other critical farm supplies were purchased on credit from Yankton Production Credit. The payment of $2,104 on 9/1/45 would have cleared the loan balance for the year, and perhaps any carryover balance from prior years.

Speculation on non-cash transactions

A few thoughts come to mind on non-cash transactions outside the probate document.

There obviously would have been a garden to raise lots of vegetables, many of which would have been canned for consumption during the winter.

The probate document presents cash transactions. Presumably there would have been barter transactions as well.

Economic Life on a Farm

There were two cash purchases of groceries, for a total of about $16. I am guessing grandma would have swapped dozens of eggs for grocery supplies which could not be grown on the farm. For example flour, sugar, baking soda, out of season vegetables, or fruits & vegetables not growable in South Dakota probably were obtained by barter.

It is my impression that more than 80 acres were worked. The cash transactions only show cash payments for 80 acres. There may have been in-kind payments for land rent. A portion of the harvest may have been paid to the landowner instead of cash.

I would guess that pigs and chickens would have been slaughtered at the farm. It is a safe guess that all the meat the family ate was from the farm.

Possibly cows might have been a bit much to handle. I would guess a full cow would be too much to store - the lack of any electricity payments suggests there would have been no frozen or cold storage to hold the beef until it could be consumed. I will guess cows would have been taken to a butcher who would have dressed out the animal in exchange for a portion of the meat or perhaps barter for other food supplies.

It is not beyond my ability to stretch and imagine that cows, or pigs, or chickens would be bartered for services the family could not provide on its own.

Observations of life on a farm in 1946

Life was hard after my grandfather passed from this vale of tears. Any way you look at the income and expenses it is obvious life was hard. Must have been really difficult for my dear paternal grandmother to raise the four kids still at home.

The narratives from my aunts and uncles make that very obvious and the dollar transactions prove it.

Farm was essentially self-contained

It is amazing how self-contained the farm was.

From the transaction detail and the other research I have done the outside inputs to the farm were gas and oil. Rain and sun provided by God. That's it. I'm guessing seed was purchased from a cooperative on credit.

The oats and hay raised were used to feed the horses. Gas powered the tractors. The horses and tractors were used to work the field to raise the oats and hay and corn.

The corn was used to feed the cows and pigs.

Some of the animals would have been eaten.

Other animals were sold to pay the cost of operating the farm.

Sure looks to me like some of the animals were sold to pay off the loan and pay the substantial cost of settling the estate.

Low productivity

The productivity would have been low. This is a time that farmers were transitioning from horses to tractors. My grandparent's farm was in the midst of that transition. Reread the narratives from the siblings and you'll see several references to the "milk sickness" that killed many of the horses and forced the transition to tractors.

An Ulvog Journey

There is no indication of fertilizer.

No specialized seed. No purchase of any seed is visible.

Possibly fertilizer and likely seed were purchased on credit. See the loan payment of $2,104 on 9/1/145 to Yankton Production Credit.

There were no high productivity tractors and none of the astoundingly high-tech equipment that is on every farm today

Cash was tight

Take a look at the detail of the costs for household expenses. I will include the coal since it would have been used to heat the house and not the barn. Here are the expenses:

date	description	amount
9/22/1945	household furniture	79.95
10/2/1945	insurance assessment	3.00
10/9/1945	Montgomery Ward, clothing	2.46
10/12/1945	Mont. Ward, clothing, repairs	12.87
1/23/1946	groceries	9.60
2/25/1946	linoleum	46.12
3/9/1946	life insurance assessment	3.00
3/27/1946	exchange on checks	0.72
	Subtotal, household expenses	157.72
2/8/1946	coal	14.00
2/9/1946	coal	23.70
	Subtotal, coal	37.70
	Total cash expenses	195.42

Purchase of coal cost $38, and that was in February or January, well into the winter.

Living expenses were $158.

Of that, $126 was for furniture for the house and new linoleum for the floor.

Of the remaining $32, notice there is under $10 of groceries purchased in a year.

The *only* clothes purchased were in the fall and that was under $16.

Take a look at expenses in December. There is nothing.

There were no purchased gifts for Christmas. There were not even clothes purchased for gifts. With grandma running the farm, four children at home, and two grown married daughters living in Sioux City there is no visible cost at all to buy anything in the Christmas time frame.

Yes, times were hard.

Economic Life on a Farm

Raising watermelons as cash crop.

One source of cash on my grandparent's farm was raising watermelons, going to town, then selling them for cash. That provided a bit of money for groceries.

Many years ago my dad and his siblings wrote down many of their recollections of growing up on the farm. Following comments from earlier in this book are used with permission.

My Aunt Louise recalled:
> "Does anybody else remember Dad loading up the wagon and going out to sell watermelons and also storing them in the oats bin for the winter? Those were the best melons—I am sure we wasted lots."

My dad remembered:
> "Dad growing watermelons on the sandy bottom land. When they were ripe, harvesting a wagon load and the next day, our Dad leaving and driving northward to sell the melons wherever he could, not coming back until the load was gone, to have some cash income."

My cousin Sonia told me the family oral history: Grandpa Daniel would raise watermelons on the Vermillion River bottom. They were easy to grow, requiring little water and little weeding. When ripe, grandpa would take a wagon into town, leaving the wagon, the melons, and a couple of the boys to sell the melons. At the end of the day, grandpa would come back to pick up the wagon, the boys, some cash, and hopefully no melons. That would provide a few dollars toward the household budget. Family members recall the watermelons were so sweet and tasty.

In those days, one had to hustle to generate a few extra dollars to feed all those hungry mouths.

We can rejoice that we don't need to sell several dozen watermelons before we can afford a trip to the grocery store.

Was living on a South Dakota farm in the 1930s closer to life in the Viking Age than what life is like today?

In recent years I have been exploring the Viking Era. You can see lots of posts on my blog (www.ancientfinances.com) about finances and technology of the time.

After looking at descriptions of life on the farm during the 1930s and in particular the economic activity we can see in my grandfather's probate document I've been wondering about life on a South Dakota farm during the 1930s and 1940s.

Did that life look more like what it would have been living on a farm in Scandinavia during the Viking Age or does it look more like the life you and I live today anywhere in the United States?

Did my dad grow up in circumstances closer to the Viking age than to now?

Let's consider the question from several directions.

Medical care

Grandma and grandpa were born on the side of the discovery of germ theory of disease transmission. Penicillin was just coming into use as my aunts and uncles were growing up on the farm.

Essentially every vaccination we currently have has come into play since my

An Ulvog Journey

aunts and uncles were born. That includes chickenpox, diphtheria, tetanus, polio, whooping cough, yellow fever, cholera, shingles, pneumonia, and now even Covid-19. Those crippling or life-threatening diseases can be prevented with a shot the cost a fraction of an hour earnings.

CAT scans, MRIs, minimally invasive surgery, patient treatment, and chemotherapy are things no one would have ever dreamt of in the 1930s.

If pills to control diabetes which are available today for pennies or maybe a dollar apiece my grandfather had been available in the 1940s my grandfather would not have died of diabetes when he did, instead he would have lived another decade or three.

Like my grandfather in the 1930s, Vikings in the 900s would have known nothing of vaccinations, advanced medical treatment. Neither my grandfather nor a Viking era farmer would have known anything about medicine to control diabetes or high blood pressure or high cholesterol or any one of dozens of other diseases which were similarly untreatable.

Standard of living

A few things that arrived on the farm after my grandfather died:

Automobiles with automatic transmission, heating/air conditioning, audio entertainment so normal that you don't need to list it as a feature on a vehicle in a probate document.

Every farmer has multiple tractors, each of which has a huge multiple of the productivity of a team of horses.

GPS controlled tractors that can plow, plant, or harvest a farmers field with the farmer touching nothing other than the start button after entering coordinates to the GPS device.

Yields on crop astronomically higher than anyone had ever dreamed of in history.

Such incredible productivity that a tiny fraction of the American population feeds all of America and a large portion of the rest of the world.

So much excess production that one would never have to dream of adopting out a child because the family did not even have food to keep another child alive.

In the Viking era families were concerned whether they had enough food to literally survive until the winter was over. Having one more or one less cow could mean the difference between seeing the spring thaw versus everyone in your family is dead by then. When my grandfather was growing up families were concerned whether they had enough food to keep everyone healthy or whether they might need to adopt out a child. Today our biggest food concern as an individual is to keep our weight under control and as a society trying to figure out how to control widespread obesity.

Instructions on how to repair any device on your farm are readily available by looking at your phone.

Electricity on every farm.

Refrigeration in every home.

Central air conditioning is most homes; swamp coolers cheaply available for the rest.

Natural gas powered central heating is normative.

Economic Life on a Farm

Never have to worry about chopping enough word to keep the house warm to keep the family from freezing to death in the midst of the winter.

Self-sufficiency

A farmer during the Viking age would raise the crops he eats, raise the sheep to spin the wool to make the clothes, and raise the animals to provide food to include milk and meat. He had to have a wife to share the chores. They needed all the children they could feed to help on the farm. He was heavily self-sufficient.

My grandfather raised the oats to feed the horses to plow the fields to raise the corn to feed the pigs and cows to provide meat to eat, milk to drink, and live animals to sell for cash income. The inputs visible in the probate document include coal to heat the house, gasoline to power the only two tractors they had, and seed.

Grandma made clothes out of the bags the seed and ground floor came in.

Everything was patched, repaired, fixed, or repurposed. Very little was thrown away because something in an item could be reused. That minimized the amount of contracted repair work and new purchases.

Farm technology

Already covered quite a bit of the factors here. Consider GPS controlled tractors which can plow or harvest an entire field without driver intervention compared to teams of horses that had to be directed every step they took.

Consider the productivity of the modern tractor compared to a team of horses for my grandfather or one mule or horse for a Viking farmer.

Consider the productivity improvement when around half of the United States was needed on the farm to feed the country compared to around 3% today which feeds the US and a large portion of the rest of the world.

When my aunts and uncles were young all the powers provided by horses. Sleeping sickness killed most of the horses and forced my grandfather to get his first tractor. Imagine the productivity increases in crops raised and the reduced time to maintain the tractors compared to horses. Compare that productivity to the several humongous, GPS controlled tractors and combines you see sitting around every farm in the North Dakota.

Conclusion

I haven't thought this through completely, but after considering merely the brief comments above on medical care, standard of living, self-sufficiency, and farm technology, it sure does seem to me that my father, his parents, and his siblings grew up in conditions that are closer to what my very distant ancestors experienced in the Viking Era than the conditions I am living in today.

Life on a South Dakota farm in the 1930s was more like life in the Viking Age than like life today.

What do you think?

www.ingramcontent.com/pod-product-compliance
Lightning Source LLC
Chambersburg PA
CBHW071519040426
42444CB00008B/1712